You Are Not Alone

Rediscovering Faith in God After Infant Loss

Dr. Nikki Watkins, LMFT

ISBN: 1977960804
ISBN 13: 9781977960801
Library of Congress Control Number: 2017916559
CreateSpace Independent Publishing Platform
North Charleston, South Carolina

Book Endorsements

"This book is a must read! If you have suffered from the loss of a child, or know someone who has, this book is for you. The author reveals her intimate feelings and "real" struggles with her process of a journey towards healing. This story is eye opening and heart-warming. I particularly loved to see how this family started to put the broken pieces of this life shattering loss back together. Celebrating Riley's "would be" Birthday is simply amazing and beautiful. What an incredible family tradition now started through something that could have easily been converted to a "sad" time every year. I am a labor and delivery nurse, and have witnessed families lose their babies before and after giving birth. Reading this book gives me a new perspective as a nurse. I believe this book can be a tool towards healing for someone who has suffered a loss of this nature. Loved ones as well as health care professionals could strongly benefit as well from gaining additional knowledge and understanding from a candid point of view. Thank God for this blessing during the turmoil!"

Kenya Moses, RN, BSN, PHN
Labor and Delivery Charge Nurse

"Dr. Nikki Watkins takes a step of courage in telling her story of the loss of her precious baby girl Riley over five years ago. Her hope in sharing her story is to help break through the stigma that continues to isolate so many families, often inhibiting their recovery. She shares with raw honesty the overwhelming grief and mourning that consumed her despite her background as a professional counselor, her strong faith and loving family support…Sharing Riley's story is another step of healing for the family and will be a source of hope for other families that read it."

Debra Cochran, Executive Director
Share Pregnancy and Infant Loss Support

"This book is a must-read for millions of couples who have suffered the pain of such an unimaginable loss. Dr. Watkins shares her amazing journey of love, joy, pain and eventually hope. By telling her story, Dr. Watkins creates a safe environment for her readers to share their own story."

Donna Rose, MA
Grief Counselor

"This was such a beautifully written memoir and will be inspiring to both families and caregivers dealing with the loss of a baby. This shows the struggle to feel normal despite all the fears and emotions you're experiencing. Thanks [to Dr. Watkins] for sharing your heartache, your spiritual walk, and your journey to a new normal. Riley is blessed with an amazing family."

Patti Budnik RN, BSN, CPLC
Bereavement Care Manager, National Share

Dedication

This book is dedicated to Riley Elizabeth Watkins, our fourth princess. Your eight months with us has transformed our lives forever. You are making an impact in this world. Because of you this book exists and will help many families along their healing journey. Thank you for inspiring us to be brave with our lives. We love you forever! See you in Heaven.

Table of Contents

Acknowledgements

$\mathcal{I}$ would like to thank my husband Greg for all of his encouragement, love, and support. He always believed in my abilities to write this book and get it published. I want to thank my three living daughters Diamond, Sydney and Noelle for their love and support as well. My daughter Diamond especially has been a big help in getting me through the publishing process and encouraging me. This story is as much their story as it is mine.

I want to thank all of my family and friends for asking me about the book as I was in the writing project and inspiring me to keep pushing forward, even when it was hard. There were many who donated money to my Go Fund Me campaign to raise funds for the editing of this book. I am grateful for you all because you helped make this God dream come true! When I was on the home stretch of my financial campaign, my mother Latisha Biggs came through with the final pledge to help me reach my goal. Thanks mom!

Thanks to my editor Lisa Abbott of Epiphany Communications who not only edited my book, but encouraged me along the way. Throughout the editing process, Lisa challenged me, stretched me, and was a constant cheerleader who wholeheartedly believed that this book would bless other families who have experienced infant and pregnancy loss. I truly believe this was a God connection and I am grateful to my cousin/sister Roz Harris for introducing me to you!

Special thanks goes to the Patti Budnik, Deborah Cochran, Kenya Moses, and Donna Rose for reviewing and endorsing this book. I appreciate your stamp of approval.

Foreword

By Greg Watkins

For the last five years, I have had a front row seat, watching tragedy break down our family's foundation and then experiencing love, as it reshaped and rebuilt our relationships. Losing our child was not very easy, and I bore as much pain and anguish as my wife. I cried with Nikki for our Riley. I celebrated with Nikki for our Riley, as we would have if our daughter were here. I continued to grieve her not being with us. The topic of infant loss is so taboo and millions of cries go unheard. For husbands, too, the experience can bring up issues like low self-worth and feelings of insufficiency and guilt.

In *You Are Not Alone*, my wife has boldly chosen to walk you through the process of our experience. She will also share stories of other individuals who have dealt with the loss of an infant. These powerful testimonies will show that YOU ARE NOT ALONE! The testimonies, lessons, and exercises can aid you in maneuvering the "new normal" that life creates after losing a child.

The pain, anger, resentment, and hopelessness you may feel are not signs of weakness. They are stages of the journey and this book will show you that today's agony can and will lessen. *You Are Not Alone* provides assistance for husbands, wives, and families to get back to the path of smiling, laughing, and living in this "new normal." We do not purport that your route will be a carbon copy of ours. What I do know, is that our experience can provide hope that there are still good days on the earth that are worth living.

It takes courage to be as transparent as Nikki and others have been, in sharing their tragedies and moments of despair in print. However, anyone suffering such heartbreak will need the same inner fortitude to seek deliverance and accept help. Many of us did not have the assistance or support we needed because we cried in private and told everyone we would be okay. So, our cries went unheard and the pain multiplied. Use this book as your cry-out-loud moment, declaring you cannot get through this by yourself. Then allow it to help with an issue that not everyone can speak to.

Introduction

One Saturday my mother-in-law stopped by our home to pick up some charity donations for her church. When I answered the door, she said, "I came to take you to lunch!" I had a feeling that God must have sent her and I did not want to pass up this blessing. Since I was still in my pajamas, I showered and dressed fast.

We sat in the restaurant for hours, talking, and she encouraged me by sharing with me her heritage and testimony of faith. I know that God sent her to minister to me and to confirm some things *for* me and *in* me. She spoke about her certainty that she has a lot more life to live because God has too much work for her to do. She spoke with confidence and assurance. When God speaks, she moves and doesn't question Him. "I wasn't always like this, but I have thirty more years of learning on you," she said. "If God tells me to do something, I obey and I *know* that He will protect me and provide everything I need." I loved hearing her bold confidence and faith in God. It was very inspiring.

I asked her if she ever experiences fear when God tells her to do something. "Sure! Sometimes He will call you to go places where you do not want to go. But I know He will provide protection," she said. Her words were an amazing confirmation of what God had spoken to me. She shared about being available to go wherever God sends, without question, because He knows what we don't know. She went on to say, "Sometimes we may miss our blessing by putting limits on what things are supposed to look like. Sometimes, what God calls us to do is not about us, but for someone else." I thought about something I once heard Joyce Meyer say; that sometimes God will call us to stay somewhere that is uncomfortable or where we think we are being treated unfairly because we are there for someone else.

As I sat there with my mother-in-law reeling from the pain I was feeling inside, she told me, "You are going to make it and be fine because God said so!" After going through one of the worst experiences in my life as a mother, I found it hard to believe her words. She told me that I needed to work through all of the feelings I had about our experience. I immediately began to cry because I would not allow myself to think about certain details. They were too painful to recall.

I felt that in order for me to move forward and on with life, I needed to push those things out of my mind and not ponder them. I knew in that moment that I needed to journal all of my feelings in order to work through my pain and grief. I also knew that my anxiety would greatly decrease once I started this process. When painful emotions came up, I kept pushing them back down. I hadn't made the connection until I spoke with Carol that day. That conversation was the start of this book.

It was amazing to see that Carol's faith in God was not shaken, even though she went through this pain with us. She was hurt and in pain just like we were, but she still could say, "God is good" and wholeheartedly trust Him. I'm sure this was neither the first nor last time that life had knocked her to her knees, but to see that she could still praise and honor God helped me to be able to do this, as well. She sees life through a glass half-full view, as opposed to a glass-half-empty view. I need to incorporate some of that perspective into my life. I wanted a more joyful way to live.

She said that she always has a song in her heart. Most times, she is optimistic and in good spirits, no matter what is going on. Her demeanor speaks to the joy of the Lord being our strength. It's a choice she has to make each day, when she wakes up. It would be easy for her to focus on all of the disappointments she has had in life, or on what is not going as she planned, but she chooses to focus on the good. We all have the ability to choose life and joy. The choice is ours, no matter how we feel. We can choose to believe, trust, and surrender again.

That day, I went home and started writing in the journal that I had been given on the day of my daughter, Riley's, funeral. The first few sentences read: *"Well, today I have finally decided to sit down and write about the thing I have been avoiding and not wanting to talk about; the thing I have not wanted to admit or acknowledge. It hurt me so deep down inside, down to my core. I have never had a pain so deep, so personal, so much a part of me."*

These sentences were the start of this book. I wrote and wrote for more than a year until my pen stopped. It is my hope that this book will bless others who have experienced a loss, just as other books carried me through my dark time. There is hope. Joy will return. And remember… you are not alone!

Part One

The Prelude

1

The Beginning

I love going to movies. They have had a way of relaxing me, since I was a little girl. I think it is because Granny, my paternal grandmother, went to the movies at least once a week when I was a kid. I was always so amazed that she would go alone and take a risk to see movies that she knew very little about.

So, when I saw the preview for *The King's Speech*, I knew I wanted to see it. I love movies that have to do with overcoming obstacles, breaking down barriers, and making a difference in the world. I also love a good autobiography because when I see that someone else was able to conquer a fear or roadblock, it gives me hope that I can, too.

I convinced my husband to go with me, even though it was not his type of movie. He likes action movies and I am the exact opposite. This film was about the prince of England, who was terrified of speaking in public. He went to a speech tutor because his fear of public speaking caused him to stutter. Eventually, he conquered his fear and gave a speech that the entire country listened to.

After the movie was over, I prayed and asked the Lord if I had any great fear like that in my life. Almost immediately, the Holy Spirit impressed upon me that I was afraid of having another child. What came next floored me. He also revealed that I would have a son to carry on my husband Greg's lineage.

I started getting hot and my heart started beating fast. We already had three beautiful daughters and I did not want to have any more children. I especially didn't want to get pregnant again! With each of my pregnancies, I had bad morning sickness. Also, my last pregnancy had ended with an emergency C-section because I had started bleeding.

At first, I didn't even tell my husband, Greg, what God had impressed on me. I didn't want to think about it and I also knew that he was not interested in having more kids. So, I pushed on, as if this new thought didn't exist, and as if the Lord hadn't spoken this to me. However, in the days that followed, it seemed that His Word to me was being confirmed.

One day, I was walking through the house, leaning backward as I was braiding my hair. Doing so caused my stomach to pooch out. My six-year-old daughter, Noelle, was on the computer in the loft. She looked at me and asked, "Are you pregnant?" Taken back by her question, I said, "No! I don't want to have any more kids." She then proceeded to say, "Did you ask God about that? You hear from Him don't you?" I stood there stunned and a bit shaken up, because I felt like God was speaking to me about this subject through my child. I never thought a six-year-old child could make me tremble in fear.

After grappling with this fear for a couple of months, I prayed to God and said that I did not want to have any area in my life that was off limits to Him. Having more children was the only area I knew of where I was not allowing Him to have full reign in my life. So, I surrendered and told God that I would have a child, if He wanted me to. As I sat quietly in my prayer closet, I sensed God speaking to me in my spirit that we would have a son and that he would be mighty in His kingdom. I finally told my husband what God had been speaking to me, and I asked him to pray about it. At first, he was a little resistant, but eventually, he said, "I can pray about it, but I've always wanted to have more kids. I could keep having kids."

And so, we began our journey of trying to get pregnant. At first, we thought we would wait until I completed my doctoral degree and found a job that paid more than I was making, working as a program director at a local homeless shelter. But once again, during my prayer time, God spoke. He said, "When I give you a commandment, it is a 'right-now' word, not a 'wait-until-a-more-convenient-time' word." I shared this with Greg, who said he had received the same word from our pastor. We began trying to conceive.

Immediately, I discontinued using my psychiatric medication, under the care of a psychiatrist, because he mentioned that it could cause possible birth defects. He did state that if it was better for me to take the meds to ensure that I stayed emotionally healthy, then I should not stop taking them right away. The last three months of a pregnancy were the most critical to discontinue taking them, due to all of the fetal development taking place. We also talked about my desire to breastfeed, and he recommended that I not take the medication in that situation. During this visit, the psychiatrist mentioned that people with a history of depression could tend to have bad postpartum depression. If I began to suffer from depression, I would have to stop breastfeeding and get back on my medication.

I really thought that I would get pregnant fairly fast, because in the past, it never took us more than two months to get pregnant, once we started trying. But month after month passed, and we were not getting pregnant. One evening, I was watching Black Entertainment Television (BET) and a gospel music family group was on. The mother was sharing her story about doctors telling her she would not be able to have children and how she had prayed and God had granted her request. She now has five children and they all sing for the Lord. She then turned to the camera and began to share with the viewing audience that someone watching was trying to conceive and would get pregnant. She said some would find out the same week, and some would take a little longer to conceive, but it would happen. That night, lying in my bed, I believed God was speaking directly to me, so I kept standing on the word God gave us.

It wasn't always easy to stand on God's promise. In addition to Noelle, we had two older daughters. Our oldest daughter was twenty years old and attending college, and our second daughter, Sydney, was fourteen years old and in her first year of high school. So many people thought we were crazy and asked, "Why would you want to start over in your forties; especially since you have an adult daughter? You guys are getting close to being able to enjoy your time alone with no kids."

As I sat quietly and meditated on God during my prayer time, the Holy Spirit revealed that we as humans came up with the concept of raising our kids and moving them out so that we could have "our" time. This concept did not originate with Him. All of our time is *His* time, and we need to do what He calls us to do. Greg and I put our trust in His plan for our lives.

At one point, we thought we were pregnant because we had a positive pregnancy test, but when I went to the doctor's office to have them confirm it, the test came back negative. The nurse decided to do a vaginal exam, to double-check. She said that my uterus felt enlarged. She asked if I had ever been told that I had fibroid tumors, and I told her, "No." She then told me it was nothing to worry about; it could be enlarged for other reasons.

After I left the doctor's office, my menstrual cycle started three days later, and we were a bit bummed out. I was convinced that I was pregnant and that during her vaginal exam, she had done something that had caused the egg to dislodge. During this particular menstrual cycle, my flow was very heavy and my cycle lasted longer than normal. I wondered if I might have had a miscarriage.

A couple of weeks later, I purchased *The Bible Cure for PMS and Mood Swings*, by Dr. Don Colbert (Siloam, 2001). In it, he mentioned that if your menstrual cycle is really heavy and lasts longer than normal, you should consider having an ultrasound done to check for fibroid tumors. I sent an email to the nurse who had performed my exam a week or so earlier, shared this information with her, and asked if she could schedule me for an ultrasound. She eagerly made an appointment for me to come in. Once I had the ultrasound done, she realized I had a fairly large fibroid tumor (7-½ cm), about the size of an orange. She said that the benign tumor could be the reason that I had not conceived, because the fibroid was preventing the egg from attaching to the uterine wall.

The nurse then scheduled an appointment for me to see a doctor who specialized in fibroids, to talk about having it surgically removed. I was excited that I finally had an answer and that we were on our way to getting pregnant soon. At this point, we had been trying for six months. We were not even thinking about conceiving because we were assuming that conception couldn't happen until after the surgery. With the holiday season approaching, the appointment was scheduled for January of 2012.

As we moved into the month of December, we planned a trip, to take the kids to Disneyland on Christmas day. My next menstrual cycle was scheduled to start a couple of days before Christmas, and I was bummed because I thought this would put a damper on my fun at Disneyland.

We had a great time at Disneyland and no menstrual cycle was in sight. I was excited when the day came and went without my "Aunt Flow," and I was able to enjoy myself fully. After returning back to our home in Chula Vista from Anaheim, a few more days passed without my period starting. I began to wonder if I was pregnant. Could I really be pregnant, even after receiving the news about the fibroid? I secretly took a pregnancy test, and it came back positive! No way! Lo and behold, I found out that we were pregnant approximately fifteen days before I was scheduled to meet with the fibroid specialist. How did this happen? As soon as we had decided to shift our focus to something else, we ended up getting pregnant. Amazing!

I kept the appointment with the fibroid specialist anyway, and he did a sonogram to confirm what our home pregnancy test already revealed. He initially wanted to do a vaginal sonogram because he said it was too early for an abdominal sonogram to detect a pregnancy. After what had happened during the vaginal exam a few months earlier, I was nervous about the idea. He thought I was making a big deal out of nothing, but he agreed to try an abdominal sonogram anyway. To his surprise, the abdominal sonogram was able to detect that I was in fact six weeks pregnant. How exciting! The kids would be ecstatic when we shared the news.

In His timing, and in spite of the physical obstacle, it seemed as though God had fulfilled His promise to us. That night in the movie theater had been the beginning of a journey we did not expect nor predict.

2

The Pregnancy

As soon as our excitement about the pregnancy began, the morning sickness kicked in. I was so sick. I stayed in bed pretty much every day, for two months straight. I was barely able to get up and make it to work. On many days, my boss had to send me home because I was walking around with a bowl, just in case my morning sickness got the best of me. When not at work, all I did was lie in bed and read. I did not talk to family or friends on the phone. I was so sick that it eventually became depressing. I enjoy eating, and not being able to eat was hard for me. When I did try to eat, my kids had to bring me food because I was too sick and weak to get it myself.

I went days without bathing or combing my hair. My husband wanted to make it all better and felt helpless because he couldn't. I just had to go through it. It would eventually be all worth it, right? I lost quite a bit of weight from not eating, and eventually started taking an anti-nausea pill in order to function. After taking the medication, I started to feel somewhat better and returned to working full time. I was blessed to have an understating boss who extended so much grace toward me, and a staff who did what they could to lighten my load.

Since the Lord had told Greg and I that we would have a son, by faith, we came up with only one name for him. He was to be named Samuel Eli Watkins. Samuel means "one who hears." Samuel was Greg's grandfather's name, and his love meant a lot to Greg, so we wanted to honor him in this way. The whole family got on board. From day one, when we spoke to or about the baby growing inside of my belly, we referred to him as Samuel or Sammy. My middle daughter even wrote his name in big letters on the bathroom mirror.

When I was approximately five months pregnant, I was scheduled to have a sonogram so we could find out the sex of the baby. Greg met me during his lunch break so that he could be in the room when the doctor confirmed what God had already spoken to our hearts; that we would have a son. So, when the technician informed us that we were going to have a girl, we were very confused.

Greg and I sat there in shock for a few minutes. We could not believe it. Greg asked the technician to check again, but the gender did not change. All we could do was look back and forth at each other in disbelief. We were not devastated because of our own personal desires to have a son, but because we wondered if we had somehow missed God. It had seemed like everywhere we went, there had been confirmation after confirmation of the name Samuel. We heard the name over and over again.

From the doctor's office lobby, we called the girls, who were in Georgia with their grandparents for spring break. We told them the news that we were having a girl. They were standing in faith with us, so they were confused, as well. We didn't have an answer for them as to why we were not pregnant with a boy, as God had said. After leaving the doctor's office, we went to our car and sat there for a while, kind of stunned.

We began to call our family members and pastor friends, to ask them what they thought this development meant and how we could have been mistaken about God's direction. We got the standard message about being thankful that the baby was healthy because so many people who want babies can't conceive. Of course, we knew that, and we were happy that she appeared to be healthy, but that was not the issue at hand. Others told us that obviously, it was God's will for us to have another girl. Clearly, they didn't understand what we were saying or going through. The news didn't line up with what God had told us. It wasn't just the fact that we weren't having a boy; it was the fact that we had been so sure about what God had spoken to us.

We chose to be thankful for the child God had blessed us with, regardless of the gender. Of course, now we had to stop calling the baby Samuel and come up with a girl's name. Greg and I both looked through many baby name lists online, and I even added a baby name app to my phone, but we had a hard time agreeing on one. The name we would give our child was important to us because every name has a meaning and each time you call the child by name, that meaning, whether good or bad, is being spoken over their lives.

I liked names that were more unisex and less traditional, like Ryan and Riley. Greg liked the name Hannah. My co-worker was expecting a baby a few months before us and was naming his daughter Hannah, so that name was out for me. Greg asked me what I thought about the name Lauryn. I thought it was different, so we settled on it. Next, we moved on to trying to find a middle name for our little girl.

I had a really loving relationship with my paternal grandmother and I wanted to honor her by somehow giving our baby a part of her name. Her name was Beatrice Elizabeth and people called her Betty. So I presented Greg with the idea of giving our baby my grandmother's middle name. Before we made a decision, I asked Greg what his grandmother's name was, because he really cherished her as well. He called his mother and found out that his grandmother's middle name was also Elizabeth. No way! How could we have been married for fifteen years and not known that our grandmothers had the same middle name? That settled it. The baby's name would be Lauryn Elizabeth. It seemed perfect to me, even though I still secretly wanted to choose Riley for a first name.

After a few months, Greg and I were having a discussion about Lauryn's name and Greg asked if there was another name that I liked more than Lauryn. I reminded him that my first choice had always been Riley. I asked him if he would consider changing her name. He agreed to think about it. Yippee! I went on Facebook and asked people which name they preferred: Lauryn or Riley? A lot of people liked both, but Riley definitely had the most votes. Greg finally agreed to go with Riley. I was super excited. So, our little girl's name was to be Riley Elizabeth Watkins. It was finally settled.

Our oldest daughter, Diamond, had always planned to call Lauryn "LoLo" for short. So, even though we changed the baby's name to Riley, Diamond continued to call her LoLo throughout the entire pregnancy. Every night, she kissed my stomach as a way of saying goodnight to LoLo. She would then go on to tell her how she couldn't wait to see her and read her a story.

Noelle was excited to finally be a big sister, and Sydney, who loves babies, wanted the opportunity to help out with the baby. We all had our own reasons for anticipating the birth of Riley. Diamond was sad that she had to go back to college in January, because she felt like the baby was going to forget her. This time during my pregnancy was such a nice bonding time for our family.

This season brought Greg and I closer together because we had so many decisions to make regarding the baby and had to work on plans for her room. Since I was pregnant, I was not able to do all of the things I could before, so Greg hung around more, to help me out. He was such a gentleman throughout the whole pregnancy. I felt so loved and cared for. It was like we were dating again. He held open doors, carried things, cleaned, cooked, etc. It was such a nice time in our lives.

Near the end of my pregnancy with our third daughter, Noelle, I began to bleed, out of nowhere. Three weeks before I was due to deliver her, I sat down to eat dinner and when I rose from the chair, there was a pool of blood. I was rushed to the hospital to have an emergency C-section because my placenta had separated from the uterus.

As a result of this prior experience and because of my age, my doctor recommended that I have monthly sonograms during Riley's pregnancy by a perinatologist. At about four months' gestation, the nurse was having a hard time getting all of the pictures she needed of Riley's heart. After an hour of trying to get a better image, she left the room to consult with the doctor. She came back and told me not to worry; they would take another look next month, when I came back.

The next month, the same thing happened. But this time, the doctor performed another sonogram himself, to see if he could get a better view of the heart. After completing his sonogram, he said he wanted me to get a second opinion from a pediatric cardiologist because it looked like the left side of Riley's heart was not growing at the same rate as the right side. I already was seeing my obstetrics and gynecology doctor (OB/GYN) and perinatologist once a month, and now another doctor had been thrown into the mix.

Greg and I went to world-renowned Rady Children's Hospital in Kearny Mesa, California, to see the pediatric cardiologist. We sat in a dark room with a nurse who spent an hour taking pictures of Riley's heart. The doctor told us that the left side of her heart was still smaller than the right side and that if the problem did not correct itself, Riley would need a series of surgeries after she was born. He also said she would likely need to be under the care of a cardiologist until she was about twenty years old. He mentioned that there might be something going on with the pulmonary valve, but that he would wait until our next visit to see how things were going.

Of course, initially we were devastated. We expected Riley to be healthy throughout the pregnancy, like the other children had been. This was a huge curve ball thrown our way. That night, at home in bed, I woke up crying over the news we had received, but Greg convinced me to have faith in God. We each decided to select a handful of trusted friends and family to pray with us for Riley's heart to be healed. We were very confident that this problem was going to be resolved before she was even born. At this point, we didn't tell the kids what was going on because we didn't want to scare or worry them.

When we returned to the doctor a month later, he said that he was not concerned about the left side of her heart not being as large as the right side anymore because even though it was still smaller, its size was within normal range. However, now he saw a problem with the pulmonary valve. It was not closing all the way, as it should. The blood was flowing out, but since the valve was not closing all the way, some of the blood was flowing back in.

He said that sometimes this problem corrects itself after birth because the blood is not flowing as fast at that point. If the problem was still present, however, Riley would need surgery shortly after birth, to place a balloon in her heart, with an incision through her belly button. The balloon would be inflated to break up whatever was keeping the valve from completely closing. The doctor said that this would likely be a one-time procedure, and she probably would not need any more surgeries.

Of course, this was still sad news for us, but it seemed like better news than what we had received at our last visit. I prayed and asked God for the grace and the strength to be able to go through this, if I had to. I couldn't imagine having to see our precious, helpless little baby go through surgery and experience pain. I wanted to spend time with Riley immediately after she was born; to enjoy skin-to-skin contact with and breastfeed her. But if they were going to take her away right after birth, I would not have this opportunity. As a psychotherapist, I was very concerned about the initial attachment I would have with my baby.

I spoke with both my OB/GYN and the pediatric cardiologist about my concern, and both assured us that we would be able to have some bonding time with Riley before they took her to the Neonatal Intensive Care Unit (NICU). We also were relieved when they assured us that Greg would be able to be present with Riley during the heart surgery since I would be in recovery from the C-section. With this news, we started working on a plan for who would stay with me while Greg was with Riley. We shared the progress report with those who were praying for us and asked them to continue to pray for Riley's healing.

As the pregnancy progressed, it seemed like one thing after another popped up. I had the glucose test that all women do when they are pregnant, and my results came back normal. However, during a routine ultrasound, the doctor said that he saw too much amniotic fluid, which could be an indication of gestational diabetes. He had me take the three-hour glucose test. I had to drink a bottle of glucose and then sit in the lab for three hours, as they drew my blood every hour. The gestational diabetes test came back negative, but we discovered that my iron levels were extremely low and that I needed to start taking 325 mg of iron a day.

Next, my OB/GYN informed me that because I was over forty and had a history of premature delivery, I would have to start going to the hospital twice a week, to check the baby's heartbeat and make sure she was thriving. We were informed that the monitoring often helps to prevent stillbirth. My husband protested because he felt like that would be too stressful for me to go to the hospital so often, but I wanted to do everything they asked us to do. So twice a week, I went to Sharp Mary Birth Hospital in Kearny Mesa for a sonogram, after which I was required to sit in a recliner chair hooked up to a heart-monitoring machine. I loved to listen to baby Riley's heartbeat.

It was inconvenient because I had to leave work early and never knew how long I would be there. Sometimes I was in and out quickly. But other times, I would be there for hours. I had to stay until her heartbeat rose above a certain level. Eventually, I got the routine down. The nurse told me to wait to eat until after she had gotten the baseline heart rate. I brought my lunch or snacks and patiently waited about ten minutes before I started eating. I could tell that Riley liked it when I ate because she would move around a lot.

As my due date got closer, I reduced my work schedule and started preparing my staff for my absence during maternity leave. I planned to be out for three months, but Greg and I were still working on a plan for me to take an extended leave of absence. I had stayed home for two years with Noelle. I knew that I couldn't take off that much time with Riley, but I wanted to be home with her for as long as I could. I did not like the idea of our baby spending more hours of the day with someone other than her parents.

Throughout the pregnancy, people blessed us so much with baby items for Riley. In late July, our friends gave us a baby shower and between the gifts, gift cards, and cash we received we were able to get everything we needed. We barely had to spend any of our own money. The only things we paid for were diapers, a rocking chair, a few gowns and socks, organic detergent, and dryer sheets. We had a closet full of new and used clothes and shoes just waiting for Riley to wear them.

The weekend after the baby shower, Greg and I went to Babies-R-Us and spent hours shopping and exchanging items. We walked around the store so long that my feet were swollen when we left. I was so excited that I had made it through the entire pregnancy, until this point, without my feet swelling. Although there had been a few bumps in the road along the way, we finally made it to the home stretch of the pregnancy. We were all elated that we were only weeks away from meeting our baby girl, Riley Elizabeth.

3

Out of the Woods

On August 3, 2012, I went to the Sharp Mary Birth Birthing Center for my regular antenatal testing appointment. I hoped the nurse was able to get a good read of Riley's heartbeat pretty quickly this time so that I would have a window of time to stop at McDonald's for lunch before my next appointment. I was scheduled to go to Rady Children's Hospital for another appointment with the pediatric cardiologist.

Just as I hoped, the first appointment was short and I was off to Micky D's! I planned to sneak and get my food before meeting Greg for our sonogram appointment. But Greg surprised me and met me in McDonald's. I love when he pops up and surprises me like that! So he sat with me as I ate my cheeseburger and fries. I really did not want to offer him any of my fries, because it was one of my favorite pregnancy treats. I know it was selfish of me, but I reasoned that I was pregnant. I offered him some anyway, secretly hoping that he would decline the offer. Of course, he did not, so I shared with him. After all of my food was gone, I was still hungry, so I asked him to order me another small fry before we headed upstairs. That did the trick!

At the hour-long appointment with the pediatric cardiologist, the technician took lots of pictures, which was not unusual. At the end of the appointment, he was having a hard time getting one last picture of a specific part of Riley's heart. After consulting with the doctor, he returned and said it was okay that he did not get the picture and that the doctor would be in shortly.

At each appointment, I had to lie on my back for a long period of time while the pictures were taken. I was always concerned about this, because every pregnant woman is told that she is not to lie on her back for extended periods of time or it could cause harm to the baby. Each time I wondered, "Why is it okay for me to do this during appointments, but not at home?" I shrugged it off and assumed the doctor would know best.

At one point as I was turning on my side to get in a more comfortable position, I had a really sharp pain in my stomach, unlike any I had felt before. I stopped and sat still for a moment until the pain passed. The sonogram technician asked if I was okay. I told him I was fine, and that it was probably just the way the baby moved in my womb.

When the doctor finally arrived, he looked very weary. We thought he had that look because something was wrong with Riley, but he said he had a long, hard day. He informed us that he reviewed the pictures of Riley's heart and her condition had remained stable since our last appointment. He was pretty sure that after Riley was born he would only need to do a sonogram of her heart to be sure that everything was okay, and then send her right back up to us.

That was encouraging news for us! We had so many people praying for Riley, so by faith, we took the doctor at his word. Greg even said, "Amen!" and held up his hand for the doctor to give him a hi-five. I laughed because that was just like Greg. The doctor looked a little uncomfortable giving Greg a hi-five, but he obliged anyway. We left there in good spirits and ready to send out the praise report to all those who were standing in agreement with us for Riley's healing. As we were getting on the elevator, I told Greg that the song from *The Wizard of Oz* came to my mind, "No bad news...don't nobody give me no bad news." We were out of the woods.

That evening, I dropped off my daughter Noelle, at the hair salon where my good friend LaShawnda worked so she could ride home with her for a sleepover. While I was there, she offered to wash my hair because I was getting it braided the next day. Of course, I accepted because I was big and pregnant and not in the mood to wash my own hair. I was already looking like a bit of a mess because I was tired. You know how it gets near the end of the pregnancy; not many things fit anymore, you don't want to spend more money on maternity clothes, and you are so tired that you do not even care what you look like. Somehow, you think you have a pregnant pass to look a bit disheveled.

As she reclined the chair back toward the bowl to shampoo my hair, I was concerned about how this posture would affect Riley. Since I was lying pretty far back, I was worried about cutting off her oxygen flow. After LaShawnda was done shampooing my hair, I strained and had a really hard time getting up. Again, I hoped that I did not do anything to harm Riley. I was thinking to myself, "I cannot keep putting stress on my belly like that."

After leaving the salon, Diamond, Sydney, and I stopped to pick up pizza for dinner. It was a fun night! We joined Greg in the family room for dinner and a family card game. I was so tired after the card game that I went straight to bed and did not do my nightly kick counts. We had no way of knowing that the very next day, our entire world would be turned upside down.

4

The News

The next morning, I woke up early, excited to go to the salon to get my hair braided. As I lie in bed adjusting my eyes to the light, I realized that I did not feel Riley moving. Many times, if I had missed monitoring my kick counts at night, I would make up for it the next morning. Riley would always start moving bright and early. I thought it was odd that I hadn't felt anything, and I spoke to her, asking her why she wasn't moving. I decided to get up and shower.

As I stood in the shower, I let the warm water run over my belly because that would usually get her moving. This time, I did not feel anything. I even started scratching my stomach because that was another tactic that normally worked. I don't know if the scratching sound bothered her or if she actually liked it, but she usually moved when I did that. Nothing. Again, I thought it was odd, but maybe I was being paranoid. At some point during the day, I was sure she was going to move.

I spent six hours at the hair salon, getting my hair braided. The whole time, I paid close attention to whether or not I felt Riley move. At one point, I thought I felt a slight move, but it was so slight that I could not tell for sure. I ate breakfast while I was at the salon and downed lunch on my way home. She usually would move while I ate, but I felt no movement.

By then, it was about 4 p.m. and it had been way too long without feeling her move. When I got home, I decided to do my kick count test again so I laid down on my side, like the paperwork from the doctor's office suggested. It said to lie on your side, especially your left side, and see if you feel any movement within a one-hour period. I rested for an hour in the bed while reading a book and there was still no movement. At that point, I was really concerned, but I was trying to stay positive.

The paper also said that if you do not feel any movement within that hour period, eat something or have something sugary and then do the test again. I did both. I went downstairs and ate some dinner with the family, drank a sugary drink, and then went back upstairs to lie down to do the test again. As I went upstairs, Greg asked where I was going and I finally had to tell him what was going on. I did not want to get him worried for nothing, so I had not told him about my concerns. I knew that if there were no movements within the next hour, the next step would be to call the hospital.

I resumed reading my book and kept looking at the clock to see when my hour was up. Greg came to check on me at one point, to see if she had moved, and I told him, "No." After the hour was officially up, I called the hospital's triage department and told them what was going on. After a series of questions, they suggested that we come in. They did not sound alarmed at all. It was more like, "Just come in because it is better to just be safe and check it out." I told Greg that we needed to go to the hospital. We had gone there other times during the pregnancy for other symptoms and each time we were sent home after several hours. We were hoping that would be the case again. Maybe I was just overreacting.

By then, it was late in the evening, so we asked Diamond to stay home and watch the younger girls. She was concerned and wanted to ride along with us. I just knew we were going to find out that everything was okay with Riley and that it would be a waste of time to pull the kids out of the comfort of home, just for that.

Greg and I drove to the hospital in silence. I needed to put on some music to alleviate the anxiety that was building in the car. I put on some worship music by Marvin Sapp, just to get us in a mode of faith and a positive frame of mind. I did not want to let fear grip me. Greg and I held hands as we drove to the hospital, as we frequently did when riding in the car together.

Once we got to the hospital, Greg dropped me off at the front entrance, and went to park the car. I sat in the lobby and waited for him to return so that we could go upstairs together. When I checked in at the desk, the security guard kept making small talk with me. I was really in no mood for it. I wanted to be short with her, but I knew that was not fair. She had no clue what was going through my mind.

I had on a t-shirt that read "PUSH" (Pray Until Something Happens). I did not even realize that I had put this shirt on; I had just grabbed something from the closet. How ironic that I was actually only 3 weeks away from delivery and had on a shirt that said "PUSH." Once Greg came in, the security guard wished us luck, like they do with everyone who goes up to triage, assuming they are on their way to deliver a baby. I certainly looked big enough for it to be delivery time. I hoped that the security guard was right.

Once upstairs, the nurse had me lay down on the bed so she could hook up the baby's heart monitor. I had been through this routine many times over the past month, so I knew how to help her position it in just the right spot to hear Riley's heartbeat. I told the nurse that usually right above my navel was the best spot to hear it, so that is where we started. She kept moving the monitor around, all over my belly. Several times, I thought I heard the faint sound of her heartbeat. After trying for a while, the nurse decided to stop checking for the heartbeat and called the doctor. I asked her if she could keep trying. She informed me that she stopped because she didn't want me to be scared. I told her to just look a little longer, which she did. Eventually, she went out to get the sonogram machine and to call the doctor in.

While we waited for the doctor, the nurse checked my blood pressure and said that it was high. She asked if it had been high my whole pregnancy. I told her no and that when they had checked my blood pressure just a day before, it was fine and within normal range. I speculated that it might be high because I was anxious about the current situation. In my heart, I feared that something else was wrong.

After waiting for a long while, the doctor finally arrived and introduced herself. She used the sonogram machine to see if she could actually see Riley's heartbeat on the screen. I was looking at the screen, too, to see if I could see the heartbeat, to ease my own anxiety. It was an older machine, so I could not really make out much. She moved the probe around on my stomach for a while and then turned to us with a somber look on her face and said, "It's not good."

I could not believe that she said those words to us. I thought I would faint or pass out. I turned to Greg, grabbed him, and said, "I can't do this!" I then turned to the doctor and began asking her, "Why, what happened?" She said that she did not know and that many times, they never find out what caused the stillbirth. I immediately asked her if she thought the stillbirth had happened because I had lain back in the salon chair the night before. She said no; that it takes a lot to harm a baby because it is so protected in the womb.

This was news I never wanted to hear. A stillbirth was one of my biggest fears. I wondered how people survived it. Now I would have to find out. I did not know what to do next. I felt numb. I felt like I wanted to wail out loud and throw a tantrum, but I was in too much shock to do any of that.

"Why me? Why us?" I wondered.

We asked the doctor how we should proceed and she suggested that we have the surgery to deliver the baby that night because she would not be on duty again until two days later.

No! I could not even *think* about having the surgery that night. It was too much of a shock and I needed time to process what had just happened. What if they had made a mistake and the baby started moving again? We needed to wait a little while. Plus, our kids were at home alone and I did not want to go into surgery without them near. I wanted to go home and tell them face-to-face what had happened and give them a chance to process it, as well. This news was going to be a huge shock to them, too. I really did not want to have to tell them.

Questions whirled through my head. What had happened? Why? There were no answers. The doctor said that there was nothing I could have done. I wanted Greg to cry because I knew he needed to. Right there in the hospital, I asked him not to be strong for me because this was not just something that had happened to me; it had happened to *us*. Immediately, he began to sob and it hurt me to the depths of my heart. I felt like I had hurt him and let him down, like somehow this was my fault.

Against the doctor's recommendation, we scheduled to return on Monday for the surgery. After the doctor left, the nurse informed us that many times, people decide to wait and come back for the surgery instead of having it immediately. That information made me feel a lot better because I was concerned about walking around with a non-living fetus in my womb.

We were numb. I felt like we were walking zombies. How do you just get up and walk out of the hospital with this news? How would we tell the girls? We drove home in silence, holding hands. Greg drove slowly because he did not want to have to tell the girls the news. When we got home and pulled into the driveway, he paused before opening the garage door. He just stopped the car, sat there, and started crying.

He said, "I don't want to go in here because I know I am going to break their hearts." It is totally against a father's nature to break his little girls' hearts, yet he had no choice. Our lives had been changed forever.

Part Two

The Aftermath

5

I Have Something to Tell You

We went in the house and called Diamond and Sydney to come sit in the family room so that we could tell them the news. We had planned to come home and tell them that everything was fine, and it was hard to know that we could not do that. Diamond came down the stairs and asked if everything was okay. We told the girls that Riley no longer had a heartbeat. Diamond immediately began to cry. Greg tried to console her and she did not want to be consoled. She did not want him to hug her; she just wanted to go off on her own. Sydney did not cry immediately, but after a few minutes, it hit her and she started crying, as well. We all cried and laid on each other for comfort. This was hard.

Noelle was already asleep upstairs, so we decided to tell her in the morning. I do not know how we even slept that night. We went to bed late and woke up early the next morning. Greg decided to call our pastor. They cried together over the news. On Sunday, our pastor announced it to our congregation and asked everyone to pray for us.

When Noelle woke up the next morning, we called everyone downstairs again so that she could have all of our support when she heard the news. She started crying and we all cried together again. She was really sad that she would not have the chance to be a big sister. I felt so much sorrow for the kids. As a parent, you always want to shield your children from pain in life, but it is not possible.

It felt kind of weird walking around all day still pregnant knowing that I had something, my baby that was not alive, inside of me. I wondered if she was turning blue while in there and if I would be able to look at her the next day.

Greg and I began making phone calls to share the news with those who were closest to us and with those who had been praying for Riley's healing. I was kind of in a fog and did not know quite what to do. How do you break this kind of news to people? I didn't know if I should start the conversation with normal pleasantries first or scream into the phone when they answered.

I broke the news to my mom, and she was very sad. She immediately made plans for her and my step-dad to fly out the next day. Her response was very comforting for me. She would not make it in time to be there when I went into surgery, but she would be there later that afternoon, after I came out of recovery.

Next, I called my friend, Felicia, to give her the news. I needed to talk to someone who could help me through this, to help me make sense of what this should look like. When I dialed her number, I was okay and I even said "Hello" in a pleasant tone. Since it was early in the morning on a Sunday, she asked me what was going on. I immediately broke down and could not talk. She said she would be right over.

She and Reggie were there within an hour. When they pulled up, Greg was already outside on his way to take the dog on a walk. Reggie walked up and gave him a big hug and Greg cried in his arms. Once Greg was able to compose himself, Reggie joined him on the walk.

Felicia came in the house and gave me a big hug and we cried together until Reggie and Greg returned from their walk. As we all sat there together, Reggie and Felicia shared some of their story of the loss of their six-week-old daughter. It was amazing to us, how even sixteen years later, they could still easily tap into their feelings of sadness over their loss, as if it had just happened. It was comforting to talk with someone who had been through a similar loss, and it helped us to not feel so alone.

Later that day, I was upstairs, folding baby clothes to pack away, when another friend arrived for a visit. When the doorbell rang, I was holding one of Riley's washcloths and crying as I remembered how much time I spent shopping for washcloths with just the right amount of plushness. My friend came upstairs and when she entered the room and saw me, she said, "I don't want to stay long. I just needed to see your face." She hugged me, cried with me, expressed her condolences, and then left.

My mother-in-law also came over. It was nice to have so many visitors because it made the day go by faster. Our final visitors for the day were our Goddaughter's family, who stopped by to show support and grieve with us. Not long after they left, our doorbell rang. When we opened the door, we found an insulated bag on our porch, filled with Gatorade, fresh watermelon, candy, magazines, and other snacks. Reggie had come back to bring some items that we might need while at the hospital. It was such a nice, thoughtful gesture that really meant a lot to us.

Food also started rolling in. This was such a blessing! We were grateful that we did not have to figure out what the kids would eat for dinner. That was one less thing for us to worry about, especially because neither Greg nor I had an appetite.

Although the day felt long, it had not felt torturous like I thought because our time was occupied with visitors and packing. Before we knew it, the day had ended and neither of us wanted to go to bed. I am really not sure how we went to sleep that night, knowing what we had to face the next day.

6

The Dreaded Day

We woke up Monday morning and neither of us wanted to get out of bed. We knew what was ahead of us and it just seemed unbearable. This was not how it was supposed to end. We had to be at the hospital at 9 a.m. for an 11 a.m. surgery. We eventually got up and finished packing our bag for the hospital, but we were moving slowly. What would I wear? I took a shower and realized this would be the last time I saw myself pregnant. When I came home, I would be empty handed. It just felt so wrong. I felt robbed and cheated.

After drying off, I asked Greg if he wanted to get one last look at my bare stomach before I got dressed. This would be it. He said, "Yes." He touched my stomach, kissed it, and then began to cry uncontrollably, from his gut. I had never heard my husband in so much pain. It hurt me to hear him cry that way. I felt like I had brought this pain upon everyone. I knew it was not true, but it was how I felt. I felt like I had let everyone down; like I had not produced. Riley was supposed to come out of me alive and whole, and that had not happened.

Although I had seen this happen to people on television, I did not personally know anyone who had gone through this same experience. It felt like some weird, freaky thing had happened to us. We had some close friends who had lost a child shortly after birth, and knew of people who had miscarriages, but not anyone who made it to nine months of pregnancy and then lost their baby before birth.

After we had packed the bag and gotten dressed, I headed downstairs. I asked the kids if anyone wanted to give my belly one final kiss. My oldest daughter, Diamond, did not, but her younger sisters, Sydney and Noelle, did. I noticed that Greg was taking a long time to come downstairs. He knew we needed to drop off the kids at our friends' home and get to the hospital by a certain time. When I left the room he had been almost dressed. What was he doing?

I learned later that he did not want to go and that it had taken everything in him to pick up that bag and head downstairs. When he finally came down, I followed him as he headed outside to load the bag in the truck. After he put the bag in the back of the truck, he fell on top of it and had another meltdown. He did not want to go. We eventually all loaded into the truck and started on our journey to our new life without Riley.

As we headed to our friends' home to drop off the girls, the sun was shining brightly, but we had heavy hearts. The ride over there was pretty quiet. My face felt like a waterfall because it was hard for me to stop the tears from falling. It was not supposed to be like this. What had happened? God had told us that we were going to have a child.

When we arrived at our friends' home, my husband, the head of our house, took his rightful position and gathered our family together in a group hug for prayer. I remember being amazed and in awe of how he could muster up the strength to say such a powerful prayer at a time when he was hurting so deeply. Just thirty minutes before that, he had been leaning on the truck crying, and now he was praying for us with such power and strength. Amazing! When we opened our eyes, my friend, LaShawnda, was standing there with tears streaming down her face. I was touched that our situation had resonated with her so deeply. I felt bad because she was crying and I was not. I was thinking that I probably should have been crying, but that it would just come when it was time. I could not make the tears come, and I could not hold them back when they arrived. Grief has a mind of its own.

LaShawnda gave Greg a folded-up piece of paper from her devotional book. I read it aloud on the way to the hospital and it was exactly what we needed that day. At the hospital, I checked in and went to the admissions office to start the paperwork. I did not have a good attitude because I did not want to be there. Once I was admitted, we were escorted to the pre-op room. I was short and snappy with the staff because I felt like I was being forced to do something that I did not want to do. The nurse asked me a series of questions and then gave me a gown to put on. Was she serious? Just like that? I guess for them, it was just another day at work.

Greg had to help me put the booties on my feet because my stomach was so big that I couldn't bend over. It felt weird asking for help and waddling around because I was not really pregnant anymore, right? That's how I felt; the pregnancy was over but I still had to struggle to get on and off the bed because my stomach was in the way. It was a huge paradox.

The nurse began intravenous fluids in my arm and asked me where I wanted to store my personal items. She did not seem to have a clear plan of how the process should work. I thought to myself, "Don't they do this all the time? Why isn't this better organized?"

Eventually, the nurse assisting with the surgery took over. She was a lot nicer and she felt a lot more solid. I was more comfortable with her.

The other two nurses in pre-op were bothering me, because I felt like they did not know what they were doing. Maybe on any other day, I would have been okay with that, but on that day, my tolerance level was low and I was not in the mood. One of Greg's close friends who had been through this experience had warned us that for him, even little things were magnified and caused him to go off on people at the hospital. Greg kept that in mind and put himself in check when he felt himself going there.

The nurses told us that after the surgery, they would bring us back to the same prep room for recovery. It was either that, or the general recovery area where moms and their newborn babies would be. Greg and I were very frustrated because on our hospital tour, we were told that in situations like ours, the moms were placed on a floor where there are no babies so that they would not hear them cry. Supposedly the hospital was being remodeled, so that floor was unavailable. I felt like they were being insensitive to our needs. Even while we were waiting to go into surgery, we could hear babies crying after being born. I told the nurse that it felt like torture. She eventually brought me some earplugs and I wore those for a while, until Greg let me listen to Gospel music on his iPad with his soundproof earphones. That was such a blessing.

While still in the pre-op room, Dr. Husky spoke to us and gave us the opportunity to ask as many questions as we wanted. At one point, she even became tearful while talking to us about it. It really touched me, seeing that she understood the pain involved in this and that it was not just another surgery for her. I also thought, "Wow, this must be a pretty bad situation if it even makes the doctor tear up."

Eventually, it was time to go into surgery. By this time, I was ready. I just wanted this to be over so that we could move on. Things would be better, I thought, if I could just get the dead baby, our baby, out of my body. It felt morbid for me to walk around with a non-living being in my body.

I was taken into the surgery room alone so that they could prepare me for surgery. They would call for Greg after the anesthesiologist gave me the epidural. They told me it would not hurt; that it would just feel like a lot of pressure. But it HURT! Really badly! It felt like pressure, it was cold, and it really burned. I was screaming and they kept asking me questions about what I was feeling and where I felt it. I was so frustrated. I was thinking, "I'm sure I'm not the only one who has told you that this hurts. And it feels like pain in my back. What else is it supposed to feel like?" I felt scared because they were acting like I was having an abnormal reaction.

It was freezing cold in the surgery room. The nurses told me that I needed to hurry and lie down and get situated in the bed before my legs started going numb. I opted to stay awake and not be put to sleep during this procedure, but because I asked the doctor so many questions he asked if I wanted to be sedated. I did not want to be put to sleep because when I had an emergency caesarean section (C-section) with the birth of our last daughter, it took me almost seven hours to completely wake up.

Although I was not sure if I would emotionally be able to handle holding Riley, or seeing her for that matter, I wanted to be awake to make that decision. I also did not want to leave Greg alone to have to deal with this by himself. This happened to both of us and we needed to go through this together.

I was nervous about what the C-section would feel like since I would be awake. The anesthesiologist explained what it would feel like, but I still had more questions. He asked me again if I wanted to be sedated. I was determined to stay away, but I was nervous. He told me that I would feel a lot of pressure during the procedure.

Greg joined me before they started the surgery. As I lay on the table, a blue drape was put up so that we could not see what was going on during the procedure. Greg sat near my head, talked to me, and sweetly tried to take my mind off of things. He talked about when we first met and when we started dating. Who knew back then, when we were just kids, that we would be here today, experiencing such heartbreak together?

My thoughts returned to Friday, just three days prior, when Greg had called and told me that he had figured out a way for me to be able to stay home longer with the baby. I was sooooo excited! I was going to be able to stay home for five to six months. We had thought that God had answered our prayers and made a way for all of this to work out. Little did we know that God was providing the finances for us to pay for Riley's funeral? But why, I wondered, did it have to happen at all? I was thanking the Lord for His provision, but at the same time, I was angry with Him for taking Riley and not allowing us to have her as a part of our lives.

After a while on the operating table, I had to let Greg know that I could not concentrate on what he was saying because I needed to focus on what the doctors were doing. I felt a lot of abdominal pressure and I was having a hard time breathing deeply because of it. The next thing I knew, Greg told me he was feeling lightheaded and might faint. I really thought he was joking, because Greg jokes a lot. I thought he was trying to get me to shift my focus. But when I looked up into his eyes, I could tell he was not joking.

I called the anesthesiologist and asked him if he could help Greg out because I had enough to focus on. I was on the operating table with a blue sheet up, numb from the chest down, surgeons cutting my stomach open, and my husband was about to faint.

I thought that maybe Greg felt faint because had looked over the blue sheet and had seen something he should not be looking at, but he said he had not. He said it was because he had fasted with me that morning (I had to fast prior to surgery). My husband is such a trooper and he loves me so much. Just the fact that he decided to go through the entire process with me from beginning to end was amazing. Later, he told me that his anxiety had gotten high because he has a fear of anesthesia and he was concerned about losing me. My frequent requests to the surgeons to be gentle with me had raised his anxiety, as well.

The anesthesiologist directed the nurses to take Greg out into the hallway. He was very firm with them so they would understand the severity of the situation. The nurses were all pretty short in stature in comparison to my husband and I remember thinking, "Who will catch him if he faints?"

In the hallway, the nurses told Greg to sit down on the floor. They gave him some juice to raise his blood sugar level and let him sit out there until he felt better. He said he wanted to get back in to me as soon as possible to make sure that I was okay.

The surgery felt pretty long to me, but Greg said that it was a lot shorter than he thought it would be. He said he was so happy when he heard the staple gun, because he knew that meant the surgery was over. After they had closed me up, Dr. Husky came and told me that everything had gone well and that Riley was beautiful. I asked her to prepare me for how Riley looked because I was very concerned that she would be gray or blue from being in my stomach so long without life in her body. She said she had good color because my body had kept her warm. I asked if she saw anything that would indicate what had happened and she said, "No, everything looked normal."

She also said that the perinatologist who had first diagnosed the problem had assisted with the surgery. He had looked at the placenta to see if he could find anything that would indicate a cause, and he could not find anything either. We were asked if we wanted to have an autopsy performed or if we wanted blood tests and a tissue sample taken to test for a chromosomal issue. We opted not to have an autopsy done, but did ask for the blood test and chromosomal study, just to try to get some answers. I did not want them to cut open Riley's body, especially if all they were going to do was confirm that she had a heart defect which had caused her to pass away.

Looking back, I cannot imagine that they did not observe her flattened nose and the thick skin on the back of her neck. Maybe they could not tell me about these features without testing to confirm a diagnosis or maybe they were trying to protect me; I'm not sure.

They wheeled me back into the same pre-op room where I had started. The same room where I had told them I could hear babies crying. I never heard one baby cry because I kept going in and out of consciousness, as a result of the anesthesia. We opted not to see Riley immediately after the surgery because I wanted to be fully alert and awake when I decided to see her. Actually, I was afraid to see my own baby. I felt bad about that, but it felt very creepy to me.

I later learned that many parents have pictures taken with their babies at this stage. I couldn't do it. Months later, when I discovered https://www.nowilaymedowntosleep.org, the free photography service provided to families with infant loss, I saw pictures of parents holding and kissing their babies. I felt so inadequate looking at them because I had not had the guts to do it. I really wish I could have. But I only did what I was capable of doing at the time, and I could not hold or kiss her. I really wish I could have.

While I was in the recovery room, the nurse kept pushing on my stomach to make sure that my uterus was doing what it was supposed to do. I kept having blood clots and I could not be transferred to a normal hospital room until that stopped and until I could move my legs on my own. Every fifteen minutes, they asked me to wiggle my toes or bend my knees. Greg was by my side the whole time.

Our first visitors were Greg's mom and my spiritual mom. I never would have expected that, because usually people are not allowed in the recovery room. God had sent two spiritually strong, praying women to be there for us during our greatest time of need, especially while my mother was travelling to get there.

One of them fanned me because I was hot, and the other one pulled out her lotion and began rubbing my feet. What an amazingly awesome experience! I thank God for sending them. I know they were praying for us when we could not pray. They were *supposed* to be there. God's timing was perfect.

I could barely keep my eyes open. I kept falling asleep, due to the medication. I wanted to stay awake so badly, but I could not control it. I felt like I was being a bad host. During this time, Greg was given a pink pouch. Inside it were Riley's footprints on a hospital birth certificate and a small white envelope that contained pictures of her.

I was so nervous to look at the photos. I think we both were. How would she look? Would she have good color? Would she look scary? Would she look deformed? Greg and I decided to take a peek at one picture, to see if we could handle it. He took the first peek and told me it was fine, so I took a look. They weren't horrible. She was really red and her body looked a bit swollen. I did not like the fact that her mouth was open and she still had a lot of white stuff on her. But I could handle it. She had on a hat and you could tell that her head was a little swollen in the back.

There were about four pictures in the envelope and we looked at all of them. We made it past the first hurdle. We did not think we would be able to handle seeing her at all. We were not quite sure if we wanted to see her little body in person, though. I was leaning more toward not seeing her, and I definitely did not want to hold her. I could not get a great look at the pictures because my eyes were kind of fuzzy from the anesthesia.

I liked the nurse in the recovery room. At one point, she had given me oxygen because she was concerned about how my vitals were looking. She was very attentive and nurturing and checked on me regularly. I did not feel like we had to navigate this alone. When they wheeled me down the hall to move me to my room on the general floor, she stood at the door, waving at me as if she was going to miss me. I was definitely going to miss her and was touched that she would take time out to see me off.

Greg's mom and my spiritual mom joined us in my hospital room. After a while, Greg went to pick up the kids. My mom and dad joined us, too. Their flight had arrived and they drove directly to the hospital.

I was very nervous about having a catheter put in, but it didn't hurt. I also had to have compression pads put on my legs to help circulate the blood, since I could not get up and walk yet. The social worker visited us and asked if we would like to see Riley. Greg and I both decided we did not want to see her, but our oldest and youngest daughters and my step-dad wanted to see her. So, we asked if she could put Riley in a separate room so that people could visit with her in private. The nurse used the room next door to ours and rolled the bassinet in there.

We were all in my room, discussing who wanted to go in and who did not and who was going to go in first. As we were going back and forth, all of a sudden, Greg spoke up and said that he was going in first. Hey, what had happened? He and I had agreed that we were not going to see her. Now he was going in? He went in first. When he came back, he told me that he was glad he had seen her and that she looked much better in person than in the pictures. He said that the pictures did not do her justice. This gave me the courage to want to see her. He said he had kissed her on the ear and that she had a nose like his and Sydney's. Throughout the pregnancy, he had wondered if her appearance would favor him.

So, one, by one, and even in pairs at times, people went in to visit with Riley. My spiritual mother Donna held her. I think she was the only one to do so. She said she had to. It is amazing how we think that our losses only affect us or our immediate family. She had talked to my belly on a regular basis during the pregnancy because she wanted to make sure that Riley knew who she was when she came out. She had also made a blanket for Riley's trip home from the hospital after her birth. Now we would never use it.

Diamond spent some alone time in the room with Riley, and then eventually, all three girls were in the room together with her. They were able to hold each other and cry together. Greg took a picture of them in there with Riley. He said that he wanted a picture of all four of his girls together. It is a very touching and precious photo. Sydney did not want to go in at first, but eventually, she did. After a while, I decided I wanted to see Riley because everyone kept coming back and saying how good she looked. We asked the nurse if we could bring Riley into the room where I was.

Once she was brought in the room, I just kept staring at her. I wanted to look at every detail possible, to try to remember her. She was wearing a hat and a pink cozy warmer. She looked nice and snug. Her eyes were closed tightly. I was too afraid to open the warmer to peek at her whole body. After seeing how red she was in the pictures, I opted not to. I kept rubbing her little cheek. I was surprised at how nice her color was and how soft her cheek was. This gesture was big for me because I had thought that I would not be able to touch her.

After she had been in the room for a while, my mom suggested that we should form a circle around Riley, pray, and then say to her what we would have wanted her to know. She started praying. I felt badly because I kept drifting in and out, due to the medication.

One by one, we went around and spoke to Riley. Again, Greg went first. He read a letter from his iPad that he wrote to her on the day that we had found out she was a girl instead of a boy. I wondered if all along, he had written that letter to read to her on this day, without even knowing it. When it was my turn, I really did not know what to say. I was having a hard time staying awake and I just kept rubbing Riley's cheek. I told her how much I loved her, how I would miss her, and how I really wanted to call her Rileykins. I told her that I had been looking forward to that and that now I would not get the chance.

My mom and Greg said that I talked to her for a long time, but I do not remember. When we were done, we had the nurse take Riley back out of the room. This was such a touching time for our family, and one I do not think any of us will ever forget.

7

The Hospital Stay

After all of the visitors left, and there was nothing to distract me from my reality, shock and disbelief set in again. I could not believe that we had actually lost our baby. What was I supposed to do now? Was I supposed to flip the channels on the television with the remote and try to find something interesting to watch? I was unsure of what to do next.

All of the nurses were sensitive to our situation and expressed their sorrow for our loss. On the outside of my hospital room door, the staff had hung a purple sign with a picture of a maple leaf with a teardrop falling on it. This symbol let the staff know that we had lost our baby and served as notice to be a little more sensitive in their interactions with us.

Cora, my nurse on the first night was great! She was funny and sensitive at the same time. Cora came in and cleaned me up from head to toe. She gently took her time, washing my whole body, and there was something soothing about that for me. It reminded me of *The Color Purple*, when Celie washed Shug Avery's body because she could not do it herself. I was at my lowest point and God had sent someone to come care for me.

Greg spent the night at the hospital with me and that was very comforting. We stayed up late watching the Olympics. The Olympic games became like a friend to me. They were always on television, day or night, even in the wee hours of the morning when I could not sleep. It was nice to have something so constant and so predictable at a time when my whole world had been rocked and nothing felt predictable or stable anymore.

I had a hard time sleeping without the television on, so we kept it on 24/7. I woke up early in the morning and watched Olympic sports that I would have never watched on my own, like equestrian riding, fencing, and race walking. A few times, I was able to watch the events live because I was up so early in the morning.

Greg came up with a system for checking in with one another, to gauge how we were doing. We would ask each other, "What number are you?" One meant horrible, three meant average/so-so/in the middle, four meant pretty good, and five meant GREAT! I thought this was a good idea, because I knew that we would all need to check in and see how the others were doing on a regular basis, in order to make it through this experience. We would need to be honest with and sensitive to one another. It also prevented us from being able to hold in our emotions and not talk about them. We told the hospital social worker about our system and she thought it was such a great idea that she would share it with other families going through a similar situation.

The next morning, I ate my first meal, after a whole day of not eating. They served me French toast, Cream of Wheat™ (which I did not eat), coffee, juice, and fruit. I was so happy to finally eat. We had another influx of visitors to the hospital and could feel the love they had for us.

Later that day the social worker came in informed us that we would need to have funeral services for Riley. Was she serious? I do not know what I thought they do with Riley's body, but I thought there was some type of system in place. I did not know that we would have to do this ourselves. We would have to actually contact the funeral home and arrange services? Wow. This was asking a lot. I thought, "It just keeps on going, huh? First, we lose our baby and all of the hopes and dreams that go along with it, and now we have to pay for a funeral that we do not want to have in the first place?" This seemed very cruel to me and once again, I felt like we were being forced to do something we did not want to do.

When the social worker tried to remind me that none of this was our fault, I began to cry. I told her that it was my job to protect Riley and that I did not/could not. She brought us the clothes that Riley had worn the day before, when she was with us, and we just stuffed them in the top of the storage cabinet. I did not want them. Also, she brought us a stuffed, weighted bear toy. The plush animal is weighted on the bottom to give moms something to hold and hug, since their arms would be longing to hold their baby. I did not want the bear either! I wanted to hold *my* baby, not some bear replacement. I could totally understand how someone who had no other children could want this to have something to hold onto, so I'm not knocking the idea. But I only wanted to hold my baby, and that was not happening for me. We also shoved the bear on the top shelf of the storage cabinet and left it there.

The girls had wanted to go back to school on this day, so in the afternoon, Greg picked up the girls from school and brought them to the hospital to see me. It was important to me that the girls see me each day, if possible. We had already had one loss. I did not want them to wonder how I was doing, too. I wanted them to see that I was okay.

While Greg was picking up the girls, our pastor came to visit me. He expressed his sympathy and we discussed the services for Riley that he agreed to officiate. The Pastor shared that his aunt had also experienced stillbirth, and that he had contacted her and asked her to pray for us. He said that she now helps other people who have gone through the same type of loss. I was really touched that he had contacted her and that she was willing to pray for us.

When Greg came back with the girls, we had a room full of guests again. Our friend Bil brought us Popeye's chicken and Michelle brought chili and cornbread for us to bring home so the family would have dinner to eat. Greg's mom, Carol, came and massaged my feet. It was nice having all of the company. It allowed us to get our minds temporarily off of our situation. The nurse kept coming in, offering me OxyContin®

for my pain, but I would not take it. She had been asking me all day to take it, but I was determined to stay awake. I was so frustrated that I had not been able to stay awake the day before, and on this day, I wanted to be alert for my guests. I waited until that evening to take the pill.

Greg stayed at the hospital until it was really late. I tried to get him to stay the night, but he decided to go home. Diamond stayed overnight with me. Once again, the television stayed on all night and the Olympic games were my friends. At one point, I called for the nurse to come help me go to the bathroom, and I was very frustrated that she would not help me up. The previous night, the nurse had assisted me, but this time, she wanted me to do it myself.

After I went to the bathroom with Diamond's help, I sat on the edge of the bed and just cried. I tried to call Greg because he told me that I could call him at any time, but he did not answer. I really did not want to talk to Diamond because I wanted to protect her from my pain. She is my child and I felt she should not be consoling me. But I could not keep it together. I was so upset that I had so much physical pain and nothing to show for it. It just did not seem fair. I really wanted morning to come so that Greg would be back.

At about 5:30 a.m. the next day, Greg texted me back and apologized for not answering my call. I accepted his apology and told him about the tough time I had the night before. I was able to move around better now and the nurse gave me permission to take a shower. It felt so good to have hot water run over my body. I was frustrated because I could tell that my milk was coming in; another cruel by-product that I had to deal with. I would have thought that my body would know that I did not have a baby and that I did not need to produce the milk.

The nurse told me not to let the water hit my breasts because it would stimulate the milk production and I definitely did not want that. After the shower, Diamond helped me to dry off the bottom part of my legs because it was hard for me to bend down, due to my incision. It was so hard for me to have her helping me, but I definitely appreciated her being there. When Greg came, I was nice and clean and he was impressed that I had gotten up and walked around. I was so happy to see him. We had experienced something so horrible together, and he was the only one who could truly understand how much pain I was in. I wanted to cling to him for support as we continued to go through it together.

I waited all day to find out whether or not I would get to go home. Part of me wanted to stay another night because I did not want to go home and start facing reality, but another part of me wanted to go home and get the healing process started; to get our lives going again. It was kind of confusing. Greg and my mom were both ready for me to come home. The nurse and doctor told me that I could stay another night, but I declined. My mom and dad were supposed to come up to the hospital that day, but they never made it. I was so frustrated because I had really wanted to see them, but I found out later that they were at my house, cleaning and getting it prepared for my arrival. How awesome.

As Greg and I visited with his mother and his sister, who had come down from Las Vegas, the doctor came in and gave me permission to go home that day. Before I left, I wanted to see Riley one more time. I did not feel right leaving the hospital without seeing her again, so the social worker made arrangements for us to do so. Greg's mom excused herself and went down to the end of the hall. We knew it was because she did not want to see Riley. She still was not ready.

I wanted to be more alert when I saw Riley this time because on the first day I had seen her, I kept falling asleep. I asked the social worker to take a peek at her first, to let me know how she looked and to see if it was okay for me to see her. I knew that Riley had been kept cold, so I was concerned about how she would look. The social worker said she looked fine, so I asked her to bring her in. Actually, she did not look as good as she had the first day. She was really cold and her cheek was a little sunken in. Her skin was not as soft as it had been.

Greg and I both agreed that this would be our last time to see Riley. I was upset that they did not put her back in the pink cozy warmer she had been in the first day. This time, they kept her wrapped up like a burrito in a pink blanket.

This was also the day that we agreed to allow the photographer to take pictures of Riley. The Social Worker told us that the photographers did a beautiful job and she highly recommended a specific volunteer photographer. We signed consent forms and asked that the pictures be taken in a separate room, so that we would not have to watch. I really did not want to see my baby naked.

The pictures would be mailed to us about a week after they were taken. Now I Lay Me Down is an organization of volunteer photographers who donate their time, talent, and resources to those who have experienced loss through stillbirth. They take photos and then send you the CD, to get your own copies made. We agreed that we would wait, until we were ready to look at the photos. I asked that the pictures only be in black and white because I knew that I did not like the way Riley's skin was so red. I also asked that they only take head and shoulder shots of her. Cara asked if we wanted her to wear anything special, and we told her no because we would only do head shots. The photo shoot was actually completed before we left the hospital.

The Social Worker was so accommodating and thoughtful and sensitive to our situation. She gave us a folder that had information on stillbirths, pamphlets for dads, and even grandparents, dealing with this type of loss, and a brochure on how to help children grieve. There was also a story in there that I still have not read yet. Cara told us about support groups and also had a discussion with us about where we would be having the funeral services. She gave us some suggestions on funeral homes, but we decided to go with Glenn Abby, since it was closer to our home and I had always thought how nice it looked whenever I drove by.

Greg was so happy when they gave us the okay to go home that he broke down and cried in his mother's and sister's arms. I asked my mother-in-law to buy a few sports bras for me, and some gel pads for my breasts. The doctor had suggested that they would help reduce the swelling as my milk came in and help dry up the supply faster. She also suggested using frozen cabbage. Leaving the hospital was bittersweet. I was ready to go, but I never thought I would be leaving without a baby. That was not how it was supposed to happen. I had envisioned myself many times being wheeled out of the hospital with my little bundle in my arms and balloons welcoming our baby girl. Greg would pull up, we would place her in her little car seat and I would ride in the back seat with her on the way home, to make sure she was okay.

Since I had gone to the hospital twice a week for antenatal testing, I had many opportunities to see happy parents and grandparents leaving the hospital with their newborn babies. I even saw a grandmother who videotaped her daughter walking with the baby to the parking garage, and I had thought it was the cutest thing. I used to smile in anticipation of me having my turn soon. Today was not supposed to look like this.

Before leaving the hospital, my doctor apologized profusely for our loss and told me there was nothing more that I could have done. She said, "You did everything I ever asked you to do. I believe if I had told you to stand on your head, you would have done it."

Before I was discharged from the hospital, Nurse Cora gave us instructions. She told Greg no "hanky panky" for six weeks. She also asked him for a big hug and called him Hercules. The doctor gave me prescriptions for Vicodin® and ibuprofen, to help with the pain.

I asked if I could be taken out a different exit than the one I had seen each time I had visited the hospital, because I knew that it would be too hard for me. They wheel chaired me out at a different exit; praise God. The nurse who was helping me was really sweet. She was a petite Filipino woman who informed me that she had been through similar circumstances. She and her husband had been pregnant three times and lost them all before they decided to stop trying. She waited with me at the exit as Greg went to get the truck. It was a nice, sunny day. She asked if I wanted to wait inside or sit in the sun. I wanted to go out into the sun and get some fresh air. I wondered how the sun could be shining and it could look like such a beautiful day outside, but my heart could be so heavy. Finally, Greg pulled up and we loaded into the car. The nurse gave me a big hug and told Diamond, "You take care of your mom." Finally, we were free and heading home.

8

Coronado

Of course that first night home, I had to sleep with the television on. I was so happy that Greg was off of work with me for three weeks. I needed him for strength and support. I knew that he was hurting too, but I still could pull on his natural, inborn strength to get me through. Many times, Greg cried as he walked our dog in the morning, or he'd stop and sit on a bench and text our assistant pastor or some other friend from church. My husband has an amazing way of being jolly and playful most of the time, and he is able to compartmentalize. He can take time out to sit and cry and be sad, but once the moment passes him by, he is able to tell a joke and make you laugh again. I love that God blessed me with him, to balance me out. Being around him gave me the sense of security that everything was going to be all right.

I have heard how some families break apart after such a tragic loss as ours, and I was mindful to pray that this would not happen to us. But truly, I never felt like it would. Praise God. I felt like we were pretty much on the same page with our grief and we made a commitment to allow the other person to feel how they felt and not try to change them or tell them how to feel.

We decided to let our kids take the rest of the week to stay home from school and be around family so that they could process their feelings. We had let them go to school on the day after the surgery and after Riley was delivered, because they had both said they wanted to. But I do not think either of them really knew how they were affected internally by the experience of Riley's death. Sydney said that when she got to school, one of her friends made a reference to something that was taking place on August 28. The mention of it made her sad and she started crying because that was Riley's due date. Noelle said she was sad because she had to explain to her teacher why she had been absent from school for a few days and then all of her friends kept telling her how sad they were for her. So Now that I was back home, it was nice for us to be together all week and to love on each other.

After a couple days being at home, I just lay in bed. Greg sat on the bed, too, using his iPad. As he made attempts at talking, I became really irritated with him. The more I lay there, the angrier I got. Eventually, I got up to go to the bathroom. I closed the bathroom door and just stood there as the anger rose.

I banged my fists on the walls. Then I fell to my knees and laid my head on the top of the toilet and began to bawl. I cried from the depths of my soul. I felt like every ounce of pain that was in me was being poured out. The whole top of the toilet was covered with mucous and tears. I do not think that I have ever cried that hard in my life. It came from my gut and my whole body shook. Greg ran in and started to console me. My mom also came in, wiped my face, hugged me, and laid my head on her chest. It felt so comforting to have my mom there with me.

I told her, "It's not fair!" She said, "I know it's not fair." She suggested that Greg take me out of the house to go get some fresh air. He said, "Let's go to the beach." I know he felt helpless.

I had my pajamas on, but I did not care. We got in the truck and he started driving. He drove the back way into Coronado. As we were driving there, we had to stop at a gas station so that I could go to the restroom. I got out in my pajamas. I knew people would think that we were homeless, based on how I was dressed. They also could have wondered if I was safe with Greg or if everything was okay because I got out with tears streaming down my face and snot coming out of my nose. Again, who cared? What did it matter?

I got back in the car and Greg continued to drive. I was glad he was taking the long way because I wanted him to just keep driving. I wanted to escape this reality. The whole time, tears just kept streaming down my face, and I could not stop them. I remembered my therapy clients saying that they did not want to start crying because they were afraid they would not stop. Before this experience, I did not understand how they could feel that way. It just did not seem logical. Now I truly understand what they meant.

We eventually made it to the beach and I was so bummed that there were a lot of people out there. It was a weeknight. Why were there so many people out? As we drove, we saw people with strollers and, of course, that was hard for me. We would never get to use the stroller that Greg had spent so much time researching. It felt cruel to have to see strollers. It seemed like they were everywhere.

We found a parking spot and decided to get out and start walking. I was still in my pajamas and had tears streaming down my face. We tried to find a bench to sit on, but they all seemed to be taken. Across the street was a big house with a huge, long, brick wall around it. Greg said, "I could pick you up and sit you on top of that wall." I said, "You can't do that! That is somebody's private property." I let out a sigh. Greg asked what was wrong. I said, "There I go, always trying to do the 'right' thing. What is the purpose in always trying to do what's right when stuff like this happens to you anyway?" Greg said, "There is a benefit to doing what is right. That's what makes you who you are."

I really was trying not to hear him. As I walked along the streets of ritzy Coronado, I was thinking how out of place I must have looked, walking on the beach in my pajamas. People had no clue what I had just been through. It made me think about how I judge people and I really have no clue what's going on in their lives. It made me think that I need to not judge others anymore. In the past, if I had seen someone walking along the beach in pajamas, I would have said, "What is wrong with them? Who comes out to the beach in pajamas?" You never know what's going on with people. Judge not lest you be judged.

Greg found a bench for us to sit on and we stayed there for hours, just staring out at the water. We could have stayed out there forever, but it got dark and cold. Greg got his jacket out of the car and wrapped it around both of us. I just lay on his chest (my safe place) and cried and cried. I did not want to go back home. I think that if I had not had kids, I would have told Greg, "Let's just pick up and go somewhere else, anywhere." I wanted to run away from reality. I knew that was not really possible, but it felt like if we could just get in the car and kept driving, we would leave the problem behind.

I saw teenagers walking down the street, laughing and having a good time. I thought, "Yeah, go ahead and laugh and enjoy life to the fullest while you can, before life really hits you, because eventually it will." I even felt a bit jealous that they were so happy and carefree. Even though we did not want to leave Coronado, we had to go back home.

The fresh air did help. After that day, I decided that laying in the bed all day was not good for me, so I made a conscious decision to get up every day and head downstairs, to be around other people so that I would not get to such a low place again.

I decided that I felt better when I got out of the house, so each day Greg and I figured out a way to do so. It felt good to get out and let the fresh air blow in my face. Several times Greg drove out to an area near our house where people sky dive. We sat in the car and watched as people loaded the plane, flew up into the air, and jumped out of the plane. I thought some of them were going to crash into the building but they never did. No matter how close they got to the building, they managed to make a safe landing. This was definitely a metaphor for our lives at that time. With the loss of Riley I came close to crashing into a figurative building of depression, but by making changes in my routine I was able to steer clear and have a softer landing.

9

Laying Riley to Rest

One of the tasks that loomed over our heads was the need to start setting up funeral services. We asked a family friend if she could call around and get some quotes for us. She was such a huge blessing for us in this area. She proceeded with finalizing the quote and setting up an appointment time for us to meet with a funeral director. Our friend spent a lot of time working with the funeral director to make sure our wishes were met, as we wanted a small gravesite service, rather than a memorial service in the chapel.

Greg really did not want to meet with the funeral director. When we got to the funeral home, he did not want to get out of the car. Eventually, we got out of the car and walked into the funeral home slowly. The lady at the front desk greeted us, expressed her condolences, and handed us a card and a small vase with one rose in it. After sitting in the lobby for a short time, we were greeted by the funeral director and his assistant.

We were escorted to a meeting room to start the process of planning a memorial service for our daughter. As they asked questions in order to fill out the death certificate for Riley, it just did not feel right. You should not be filling out a death certificate for your baby.

Greg was very grouchy during the whole process and was snappy and short-tempered with the guy. I knew it was because he was sad and hurting and did not want to be there, so I answered most of the questions and handled filling in the paperwork. I tried to smooth over Greg's harsh answers.

I was very surprised at how expensive everything was. I kept feeling like they were wrong to charge so much money for something like this. We did not choose this. We did not even want to do this, and they wanted us to pay this much money? Shouldn't this be free to people in our situation? Thankfully, God touched the hearts of family and friends to donate money to assist in paying for Riley's funeral expenses.

I wished that we could just stop the world for a while, so that we could deal with our situation, get a better grip on our emotions, and figure out how we were going to move forward. We had been knocked down to our knees and just needed a minute to get our bearings and get back up. But no, life kept on going and did not seem to care that we were hurting.

After we had made all of the preliminary funeral arrangements, Greg and I left a check for the fees and asked my parents, who were with us for support, to stay to choose the casket and flowers. That was just too much for us to handle. How sad to see such a tiny casket. It should not be like this. My mom also volunteered to pay to have flowers placed on top of the casket at the funeral. We were grateful they took this task off of our hands, knowing they were hurting also from the loss of their granddaughter.

When my parents returned to our house, they told us that everything had gone well. My mom said it had not been as hard as she had thought it would be. She said that the casket was really beautiful and actually did not look like a casket. It had a case over the top of it that snaps on, kind of like a sewing machine case. She had picked out pretty flowers, too. I was glad that it had gone well and was not creepy.

The funeral director sent my parents with a book for us to look through, in order to choose a memorial marker for Riley's gravesite.

Greg did not even want to look at it, so he put it on the floor next to the large chair in our bedroom. My mom also mentioned that we needed to select an outfit for Riley to be buried in. She offered to purchase one and take it to the funeral home for us.

Diamond and I had selected two outfits when we were packing up Riley's belongings and saved them for this occasion. I let my mom pick between the two. One was a cute Pocahontas dress that I loved and was excited for Riley to wear. The other was a cute, pink top and bloomer set that one of our family friends gave us. Their daughter had worn it when she was a baby. My mom picked this one. It was special that some close family friends who had gone through the whole pregnancy with us were now a part of Riley's burial.

We scheduled the funeral for two o'clock on a Friday afternoon. We would have to take the girls out of school again on that day. We decided to not open the service up to everyone; only to our close friends and family who had been on this journey with us from the beginning. That night, I sent out an email invitation to them, with the details of the funeral service.

The night before the funeral, I sent our pastor a run-down of what we wanted to take place during the services. We did not plan on having any songs or even speaking. Neither of us felt like we had anything to say, since we had said what we needed to say to Riley at the hospital. On the day of the funeral, I woke up pretty early. As soon as I awakened, I had words that I wanted to speak. I knew that the Lord had given them to me, even though I was still angry with Him for not healing Riley. He gave me words to say to our friends and family in attendance, thanking them for being with us throughout the whole process, from beginning to end. I was so surprised because I had thought that I did not have anything to say.

Greg lay in bed a long time that morning because he did not want to go. We had agreed to have a limo pick us up and drive us to the funeral home because I figured it would be hard for Greg to make that drive. I'm so glad we had made these arrangements ahead of time, because he did not want go at all, let alone drive there.

We decided not to wear black and not to get too dressed up. I still could not wear heels, so I wore flat sandals with a long, aqua-colored skirt and a white jacket. Greg wore slacks and a short-sleeved golf shirt. Diamond wore a blue dress and some flat sandals, and Sydney wore Diamond's brown-wedged sandals and a short cream dress. My mom also dressed down, with jeans and a nice blouse.

The car came to pick us up at 1:15 p.m. When we pulled up at the gravesite, the Hearst was parked directly in front of us. I don't know why, but a Hearst never crossed my mind. As soon as Greg saw it, he did not do well. When we got out of the car, he was immediately in an agitated mood. I could tell he was not in a good place. He wore his sunglasses the whole time, so I could not see his eyes. Our pastor pulled up right after we arrived which was good. Greg hugged him and began to cry.

The funeral workers told us to let them know when we were ready to have them bring Riley out of the Hearst and place her on the platform at the gravesite. We wanted to wait until the guests arrived to take it out, but Greg did motion me over to take a quick peek into the Hearst to see our daughter's casket. As we were looking inside, my mother-in-law arrived.

She wore all black and was crying very hard. She was also having a hard time walking. I had *never* seen her like that. She was a New Yorker to the core and the only other time I had seen her in this state was when her own mother died. I went over to give her a hug and to console her. It was hard because I knew that we were the ones to be consoled, but I had to console someone else.

Eventually, we had them take the casket out and place it in front of us. My mom was right; the casket was beautiful. It was a cream marble encasement that actually looked like a beautiful box. It did not look like a casket at all, which was really helpful. My parents selected a beautiful floral arrangement to lay on top with pink and white baby roses with baby's breath and lots of greenery.

Our pastor opened up with a prayer and the Assistant Pastor read a scripture. As the Scriptures were read, I was surprised at how many times he fumbled over his words. Maybe it was because 21 years prior he was standing in our same shoes.

After the start of the service, our pastor expressed how much he loved our family and said something that I needed to hear. He told me, "You hear from God." He shared several things I had told him that have come to pass in his life. I *really* needed to hear that, because I was wondering if I had heard wrong, in thinking that God had told us to get pregnant.

Next, Pastor opened up the floor for others to come up and speak. I got up to speak and Greg came and stood with me. I did pretty well until I got about half way through the speech. Here's what God gave me that morning to say:

> "We had our time with Riley at the hospital and shared with her how much we loved her and the dreams we had for her that will not come to pass. We all had so much love for her and we were waiting to shower her with it. She brought us so much joy as a family during the pregnancy. We all had nicknames for her: Rileykins, Riles, Lolo, RiRi, and little Betty. We will miss her, but we will never forget her. She will always be our daughter, sister, granddaughter, and niece and we plan to find ways to keep her memory alive.
>
> Family and friends, we want to say thank you for all of your support. All of you have been a support to us from the very beginning. From believing God with us when He told us to have another child, to praying for me when I was sick in the bed with morning sickness, to praying for God to heal Riley's heart condition, to celebrating her arrival at the shower, to crying with us when we got the news that she was no longer with us, to supporting us emotionally and financially as we mourned and prepared for this day. In this day and age, it's rare for people to give of themselves as much as you all have. You have lived out the following scriptures: 'My little children, let us not love in word or in tongue, but in deed and in truth' (1 John 3:18) and 'Rejoice with them that do rejoice, and weep with them that weep' (Romans 12:15). May God return unto you in your time of need all that you have given us."

At the end, the funeral workers asked if we wanted to watch Riley be lowered down into the ground. At first, we said we did not want to be there, but then we changed our minds. All of us stayed for this part of the service except Diamond. It was too much for her.

After Riley's casket had been lowered down into the ground, we just sat there for a long time. I laid my head on Greg's shoulder and we just held each other. The funeral workers said we could stay as long as we liked. Eventually, Greg said we needed to go because he could just sit there all day.

We invited everyone back to our house after the funeral for food and fellowship. On the way home, we were joking and laughing and I was thinking that the driver must have been wondering what was wrong with us. How could we be laughing and joking after just experiencing something so traumatic? Maybe we had cried so much at the funeral that we needed to laugh and find something fun to talk about. When we arrived home, the driver got out and walked around the car to speak with us. He told us that he had experienced the same type of loss and that the most important thing was for us to communicate and to talk to one another about how we are feeling. Amazing! Another person who had been through our same experience and had made it.

Inside the house, friends who lovingly transformed our kitchen and created a beautiful spread of food for us to enjoy greeted us. Some members of the church we were attending at the time had prepared the food. It included two huge pans of lasagna (Greg's favorite dish), garlic bread, salad, a fruit platter, sparkling lemonade, and red velvet cake. Yummy. It was so nice to sit down and fellowship, now that everything was over.

As the difficult day came to an end, our assistant pastor's wife presented me with a journal she had received at a women's conference where she had spoken. She felt led to give it to me. She called it my Riley Journal. Initially, I was not sure if I would ever write in it. Little did I know that I would fill the journal with notes that would serve as the start of this book.

Weeks later the funeral director called to see if we had a chance to look through the memorial marker book. After a few attempts, I was able to get Greg to sit down with me to look through the book. We settled on a marker with a ribbon banner across the top that says, "Our fourth princess." Underneath it says, "Riley E. Watkins, August 6, 2012." In the bottom corner is a picture of a little angel sitting with a lamb.

Once we made this choice, we scheduled an appointment to meet with the funeral director to finalize the details. Of course, Greg had no desire to go back to the funeral home. My mom and our oldest daughter Diamond went with us, and when we got there, Greg did not want to get out of the car again. Once we finally got him inside, he did not want to engage in any small talk. He was in a bad mood and very short-tempered with the funeral director. I decided to answer all of the questions before Greg had a chance. I totally understood where Greg was coming from, but the funeral director did not have anything to do with our loss, so I felt that he should not have to bear the brunt of it, either.

Dealing with the funeral director was very frustrating because he was trying to be overly accommodating, to the point that he was not answering any of my questions directly. Everything was, "Whatever you want." I thought, "Can you just give me an answer and then let me ask for what I want?" We also had to select the type of granite we wanted. There were some that would eventually just look like concrete after time and some that would get ruined from the water of the sprinklers. We selected one that was pretty but that would also stand the elements pretty well. It was a pretty brick color. I never would have thought of getting one in that color, but actually, in the end, I really liked it. It was a nice bold color that would make her marker easy to spot, and it kind of matches the color of the tree we planted in our yard in her honor. We learned that whenever we planned to visit the cemetery, we could call ahead of time and ask them to clean off her marker. I thought that was very thoughtful. At the end of the appointment, we were informed it would be approximately four months before the marker would be placed on her gravesite.

When we left the funeral home office, we decided to stop at Riley's gravesite. Greg was having a very hard time and did not want to stay long. He just stood by the side of the car and cried. My mother, Diamond, and I walked over to Riley's gravesite to see it for the first time since the funeral. Diamond knelt down and just talked to her sister. She didn't want to leave. At first, I told my mother how hard it was to think of Riley being down in the ground, but she reminded me that only her shell was buried. She is a spirit and her spirit was in heaven with God. That helped me not to think of Riley just lying in the ground.

Before leaving, the three of us walked around the area where Riley was buried called Kiddyland. It was an area of the cemetery sectioned off with a white picket fence painted with small handprints and kites. There were a lot of windmills and balloons placed on gravesites by loved ones in remembrance. We began to read the markers of some of the other babies there. It was so sad to see families that had multiple losses, and some less than a year apart. I actually prayed for some of them. I couldn't even imagine trying over and over again and losing multiple babies. Those were brave people.

Some of them had miniature gates around their marker. Greg said he wanted to do that for Riley and that he would go to Home Depot to purchase one. Finally, we left, and Greg was pretty quiet the rest of the way home. I was happy that we had finally finished the whole business of the gravesite. It was another thing we needed to conquer so that we could continue our journey of healing.

10

Baby Stuff

After Riley passed away, we rushed to put all of her belongings in the garage so that we would not have to look at them. We stored everything in a corner and draped it with sheets so that we wouldn't see it. The fact that we were storing these items in the garage instead of using them for our baby felt like a nightmare.

It was definitely easier to have everything covered up, but of course, each time we saw the sheets, we knew what was underneath. One time I went out to the garage to get something, and got a whiff of baby powder from the dryer sheets I had bought for Riley. Even though it was out of sight, I was reminded about what had happened, just by the smell.

For a long time, Greg and I didn't want to deal with the stuff in the garage. Many people offered to help us get rid of the items and take them back to Babies"R"Us®, but we just weren't ready to deal with it at all yet. We didn't want to have to sift through the items and conjure up our sad feelings. Finally, one day, about a month after Riley's passing, Greg decided to put some of the items on Craig's List, to try to sell them. Someone contacted him to purchase the rocking chair, and Greg informed me that the buyers would be coming by within a few days.

I didn't really think much of it and was actually happy that we were starting to get some of the stuff moved out. But I didn't expect the flood of emotions that would come when I walked into the garage and saw the rocking chair and ottoman sitting in the middle of the floor. Reality hit me. That was the chair that we had spent so much time searching for because we had wanted a nice one, but didn't want to spend hundreds of dollars. We had found the one we wanted on Craig's List, for half the store price. We had been so happy about that. Now it was being sold on Craig's List again and I had never had the chance to rock Riley in it.

When the couple came to pick up the chair, I was walking back from the mailbox and saw them slowly stop in front of our house. At first, I was confused as to why they were coming over, but then I remembered that someone was supposed to purchase the rocking chair. I told them that I would go get my husband. At first, I was going to just let Greg completely handle it, but for some reason, I ended up going out in the garage to join them. I really do not know why I went out there. They did not take long to decide they wanted it, and before I knew it, the father-to-be and Greg were both loading the chair and ottoman in the couple's van. Just like that, it was gone and Greg was walking back with $150 cash in his hand. He had a smile on his face because he had sold it, and I went upstairs with an ache in my heart.

We had made plans to join some family friends at a high school football game that evening. I went upstairs to get dressed for the game and ended up lying on the floor in my closet with the door closed. I was emotionally drained from the rocking chair incident. I just lay on the floor and cried again for the loss of our Riley. I don't know how long I stayed there, but when I finally got up, it took me a long time to pick out my clothes and get dressed. I knew that Greg was downstairs waiting on me, but I was struggling.

When I finally went downstairs, it was dark outside and past the time we had agreed to leave the house. Greg asked me if I had been upstairs in the closet crying, and I told him yes. I asked how he knew, and he said he figured that's what I had been doing, since I had taken so long. He said he would not have told me about the rocking chair if he had known that it would upset me. I didn't know in advance that it would upset me, so I couldn't have shared that with him.

We went on to the game, but I was in a lousy mood for the rest of the evening. I was not very talkative with our friends and was actually a bit on edge and snappy. I could tell Greg was a little frustrated by my irritable mood, but he gave me my space because he knew why I was upset. I didn't feel like sharing with our friends what was wrong, so I just kept to myself most of the evening.

A family friend helped me to get rid of Riley's clothes by selling them at a consignment store. There were two boxes of clothes, blankets, and infant diapers. I just couldn't bring myself to look through the boxes, so I gave them to her as they were. She was able to sell most of the items. I really appreciated her help

Her husband, who is also Greg's fraternity brother, offered to take back all of the items that we had purchased from Babies"R"Us®; the stroller, bathtub, bottles, lotions, and other items. He told Greg that at first, the store didn't want to give him cash back, since we had used gift cards for a lot of the purchases. But he spoke with a manager, informed him of our situation, and was able to get close to $500 in cash and $150 in gift cards that we could use at Toys"R"Us® for Christmas gifts for our kids. That was a huge blessing and helped to move out a large chunk of our inventory in the garage. It was nice to see the pile shrinking each time I walked into the garage.

It had been four months since Riley passed and I was finally able to look at what was left under the sheet. This was a big deal for me. It brought back so many memories. As I looked through the items, the Holy Spirit impressed upon me to start blessing other people in need with the belongings Riley would never use. Soon after, I became aware of other people in need. We gave wipes, diapers, baby laundry detergent, dryer sheets, baby hangers, and a baby doll to our goddaughter who was still a toddler at the time.

Then, I saw a lady at church who already had three small children and was pregnant with twins. I knew they were struggling financially. I thought that we could bless them with the stuff we tried to sell but could not. Her husband came over and we gave them the crib, pack-and-play, swing, baby rocker, high chair, and a few other items that were left in the garage. He was very appreciative and so were we. They were having twin boys, so some of the items were a bit too girly, but they knew of a young high school girl who was having a girl soon and they said they would give the items to her. A few days later, I noticed that Greg still had my maternity clothes in the trunk of his car and I decided to give them to this young mom-to-be, as well. She was smaller than me, but since she was having twins, she was growing out of her clothes at a rapid rate. She said she felt honored that I would give these items to her.

Now the garage was empty. It was nice to have everything gone, but on the other hand, it made everything final and real. Now pretty much any attachment to Riley was invisible. Even my mother said she felt sad when she went in the garage and didn't see the pile under the sheets.

We kept a few of Riley's keepsake items; baby shower pictures, the wooden letters someone had given us that spelled Riley's name, and a pair of cute little socks with flowers. I saved a picture we had taken of Greg and me together while I was pregnant, with my belly exposed and our hands together, making the shape of a heart over my belly button. I saved the framed scripture from my daughter, Diamond, about God answering our prayer for a child.

I kept trying to find ways to keep Riley's memory alive. I had so many ideas about what I wanted to do. First, I searched online for a necklace. There were so many nice options. I could get her initial on a chain, an engraved bar with her birthday and name, a pendant with little footprints, a teardrop, or a mom holding a baby. I came across a necklace that I really liked, but I just didn't feel peace about ordering it. Greg decided that he was going to get a dog tag-style necklace with Riley's name and birthdate on it.

Next, I searched for car memorial stickers; maybe an angel or little baby feet with Riley's name and birthdate. I kept switching from idea to idea and not settling on anything. I wanted to do something, but really didn't know what.

Eventually, we settled on planting a "Riley tree" in our backyard. I really wanted something that had some color to it; something unique and not an ordinary green tree. As we walked the aisles of the garden section in the store it didn't take us long to make a decision. As soon as I saw the red plum tree, I knew that it was the one. The leaves were a vibrant, rich, plum color.

We planted the tree in the corner of our backyard on September 6, 2012; exactly one month after Riley had been delivered. Just a day later, I received a text from a family friend who had something for us that they wanted to drop off. We came home and there was a tree on our porch! They had purchased it for us to plant in our yard, in memory of Riley. And get this; it was a fruit-bearing plum tree! Our friends attached a card, saying they had one of the trees in their yard and that each year it bears the most amazingly sweet fruit. So, each year when the tree bears fruit, we eat a piece of it and think of our sweet Riley. Oh, I miss her so.

I also decided to purchase a special box to put some of her items in. I found the perfect one at a craft store. It had the word "love" written all over it and the characteristics of love. It was a very girly pink, beige, and red, with roses on it. I planned to keep it in the garage so that we could look in it when we wanted to, but Greg wanted to keep it in our dining room on the credenza. I didn't know how I felt about the idea, but I thought it was worth a try, since Greg usually didn't want to have things around as a reminder of Riley.

On the same day that I purchased the keepsake box, I also purchased a beautiful frame for the family picture that we had taken on Father's Day. It is the only picture we will ever have of us as a complete family. We planned to display it in the upstairs hallway. Greg agreed that we should hang it up, but he wasn't ready yet for us to do so. I asked the girls if they would be okay with the picture up there and everyone agreed that eventually it will be okay, but not yet. The framed picture stayed behind the couch in the loft for almost four years before everyone was comfortable with it hanging on the wall, near all of our other family pictures.

When we discarded Riley's belongings, I saved a couple of bags of baby clothes and planned to have a quilt made from them. My mother-in-law gave me some quilting templates so that I could cut out squares of material. Usually, I did this in the evening while watching television with Greg, but he said it was hard for him to see me with her clothes. I eventually stopped this project since it was hard to find a time when Greg and I were apart long enough for me to make significant progress. Instead, the clothes stayed in my closet for about a year. I learned about a girl in the Dominican Republic who was having a baby as a result of sex trafficking and had no clothes for the soon-to-be born baby. I decided it was time to release Riley's clothes and gave them to her, with the hope that they would be a blessing.

We experienced so many conflicting emotions throughout this whole process. We felt blessed that we were able to help a single, teenaged mother with some much-needed clothing. We were equally grateful that we could bless another family who was having twins (their fourth and fifth children) with baby furniture. But there was also sadness that Riley would not sleep in her crib or wear all of the cute clothing. In the midst of our grief, we knew that God was using us to bless others in need.

11

Party Time

It's so interesting how life just keeps going, no matter what you are going through. We wanted time to just stop for a while so that we could get our bearings, but of course, that did not happen. About two weeks after Riley passed, our older girls' birthdays came around. We had to, and wanted to, celebrate. We didn't want them to feel like their birthdays were not important and it gave us something joyful to focus on.

We celebrated Sydney's birthday over dinner at a Japanese restaurant. That evening, it took everything in me to appear happy. I was so sad on the inside. I was really not in a good mood. It had been a rough day emotionally, and I barely was able to get myself together enough to leave the house and go to dinner. I had written in my journal earlier that day:

> *Today is Sydney's fifteenth birthday. The song that keeps rolling in my spirit is "It is Well With My Soul" by Mary Mary. I do not feel like it is well with my soul right now. I'm not okay with what happened. I'm not okay with Riley not being here in an earth suit with us. I want to see her, touch her,*

kiss her, love on her, and call her nicknames. We miss her. She was with us for a little over eight-and-a-half months; such a long time to then lose her. It's hard for me to be happy for others who are pregnant and joyful. I feel robbed and cheated. This doesn't seem normal. I can't understand if it was purposed or just a fluke? It's sad...I'm sad. I feel like my world got rocked. I feel like everything I knew for sure feels unsure, unpredictable, and uncontrollable.

Later in the day, I wrote another journal entry:

I'm frustrated because everything makes me irritable and cranky and I'm easily stressed out and frustrated. I don't like living like this, I don't feel like I have a good quality of life like this. I'm touchy and sensitive and I don't know when this will change. I feel really lonely and alone. I'm sure no one wants to be around me right now. I don't even want to be around myself. I don't feel like talking to others, so I just isolate myself by coming to my room. I don't know how long this will last or how to change it. I'm sure my husband is tired of me. It's amazing to me how he can be so consistent and even-keeled. I wish I could be more like that.

Sometimes I get so frustrated with how I'm wired. I need everything to be perfect and right and organized and in its place. What else is there to do but organize? I don't know what else to do with myself. I'm wondering if I need to be on meds again. I get so easily frustrated with my kids and it's not fair. I don't even like me right now and I don't want to be around myself. It is a horrible feeling to not want to be in your own skin.

I feel like my life has been turned upside down. I'm probably depressed. I had done such a good job of letting things go and releasing control and trusting God to handle everything, of not making a big deal out of small things. But I don't know how to do that anymore. I feel like I have taken matters back into my own hands to control everything again. I had given it all to God completely and then this happened. It feels like the 'Great Sadness' in the book, The Shack.

I feel spiritually lost. I gave all of myself to God and now I don't know what to do with myself. I feel lost in the middle. I can't go back to where

I was with Him, and I don't know where to go. I feel shaken, rocked, off balance. I can't trust Him or me. What do I do? Whom can I turn to? He was my best friend. I used to talk to Him all day, every day. I tried my best to please Him and do whatever He asked me to do, according to His ways. I tried really hard.

I struggled and fought with myself and died to my flesh. Now I feel like I've lost Him, like He let me down, betrayed me, hurt my feelings, left me out there. I feel tricked, bamboozled, lost, and lonely. My friend has left me. He doesn't speak to me or tell me what to do and how to live. What do I do with this? How do I go on, move forward? How will I have a relation- ship again, trust again, and give of myself again?

I feel broken, wounded, and useless. People are going to get tired of me being sad, not calling, not wanting to talk, mad at God. They'll want me to get over it. How long will this last? I see no hope, no way out. I can smile or laugh on the outside, but I'm really hurting on the inside; deep inside, way down in there.

Should I go back to school? I only went because He led me to. I have no personal aspirations. I don't even know what I'd do with the degree be- cause I was following His lead. Now we aren't friends anymore. We aren't walking together. I can't even hear Him. It was a blind faith that said, 'I'll do whatever you say.' Now I'm having a hard time with that. I'm so angry. Finishing my degree really seems like a waste of time.

Am I just throwing a tantrum? Should I just suck it up and move on? Just deal with it? No baby clothes, no diapers, no crib, no hugging, kissing, cooing, and preparations. Just four more days from now, we would have all been so excited in anticipating playing with Riley. Others have moved on, but how long will I stay here? How long is okay? Why are others able to be okay and not me? I feel so weak, so damaged, so broken and worthless. I'm an emotional wreck, trying to have some semblance of control.

At this point, my mom came in the room to check on me. I was sitting on the bed writing and sobbing. She asked what she could do to help and I told her there was nothing. She wiped my face and nose with a tissue as I cried and poured out my hurts to her. She just listened and kept saying,

"I know, I know." It hurt her to see me hurting and not be able to fix it. Eventually, she helped me get myself together enough so that we could go out to dinner.

Just four days later was Diamond's twenty-first birthday and we wanted to make it special for her. I didn't realize it at the time, but Diamond's birthday was Riley's due date. I think that, maybe subconsciously, I was grieving because of that. At the restaurant, I had a horrible headache and had a hard time enjoying myself and engaging in conversation. I could tell Greg was frustrated with me because of my mood, but I could not get it together.

Especially on their birthdays, I did not want my daughters to feel that Riley was more important than them or that because we were grieving, everything had to stop. I was trying to keep things as normal for them as possible, even though I knew on the inside I was not normal at all. I wondered if things would never be "normal" again.

12

God Kept Us Occupied with Projects

Prior to Riley's anticipated arrival, Greg had an idea about how we could access some additional finances to meet our needs while I would be on maternity leave from my job. At the time, we assumed we would use those funds so that I could have an extended maternity leave. But as things turned out, we used the money to pay for Riley's funeral, pay off some bills, and do some home improvements.

Around the same time, Greg received a job promotion and a raise. Even though I was still feeling confused about God's goodness, I knew that God had brought this additional financial blessing to us at this very time to raise our spirits. It was not a coincidence. The extra money was a blessing that came at just the right time, because after Riley's death, both Greg and I needed something else to focus on besides our grief.

First, we gathered all of our bills and figured out which debts made the most sense to pay off. Which ones would remove some hefty monthly payments, increase our expendable cash, and give us the ability to pay down on our student loans? We decided to pay off four credit cards. Greg began a bargaining process with each creditor, asking them to knock off a portion of the balance since we were paying it off with cash. It was a great distraction for him and I believe that it gave him back a sense of empowerment.

We also paid off a tax bill, not knowing then that due to an error, the payments were being applied to the wrong tax year. As a result of this misunderstanding, I had received a letter from my employer, just a few days after I returned home from the hospital, saying that my paycheck was going to be garnished. Are you serious? It felt like I was being kicked while I was down. We could not afford for my checks to be garnished. Eventually, we figured it all out and were able to pay off that tax bill. Thank you, Jesus.

Next we started our home improvements. We met with landscapers for quotes on getting our patio cemented. Through one of his friends, Greg found out about a guy who would do the work below our price range. He showed us his samples book and his work looked great. He wanted to start working right away, so Greg and I went on multiple, adventure-filled trips to Home Depot and Lowe's. We picked out palm trees and wood chips to line the patio area. These trips were actually fun. They gave us a sense of purpose and something to fill our time. Who knew there were so many varieties of wood chips, including rubber wood chips?

Greg and I bought some stain to paint the outer edge of the concrete, to give it a nice contrast. It was a nice joint project for us, sitting out there and painting together. A few times, I even let Noelle come out and help. On the days when I was severely depressed, the driveway project was a nice distraction from the black hole of pain I felt inside of my chest. I could just sit and paint. It gave me something to do that did not require much thought, energy, or effort.

With the patio done, the queen palm trees planted, and the wood chips down, we decided to buy rocks to go around the base of the trees; another fun adventure shopping trip. We had planned to lay down the desert river rocks together, however, one day I was home alone with nothing to do and decided to do it myself. I actually enjoyed the project and the solitude of working alone.

These projects took months to complete and kept our hands busy and our minds occupied. Without the energy to do much else, they brought some much-needed structure to the chaos and lack of control we were feeling in our lives due to the loss of Riley.

13

My Trip to Mississippi

After we completed our home improvement projects, I decided to take advantage of the time off from work and take a trip to Mississippi to see my ninety-year-old grandmother, whom I had not seen in a few years. I knew she was declining cognitively because my mom had been going to care for her twice a month and had kept me updated on how she was doing. I was not sure how much longer my grandmother would be around, so I wanted to get another visit in with her. I had wanted to go while I was pregnant, but by the time I made the decision to go, I felt that I was too far along in my pregnancy to fly.

Now that I was able to travel, I flew to Georgia, where my mom and stepdad picked me up from the airport. We went to my mother's house and I got settled into one of the rooms. I always love going to my mother's house without my kids because it gives me the opportunity to be a kid again, in a sense. I slept really well the first night. I was excited because I thought that I was finally free from the frequent nightmares I had been experiencing.

The next morning, we started the five-hour drive to visit my extended family in Mississippi. I looked forward to this uninterrupted time of refreshment, to read and listen to God's Word on my phone.

I was so excited when we finally made it to Laurel, Mississippi. It felt like coming home. When we pulled into the driveway, my Uncle Stanley greeted us. I was happy to see him looking healthy, because the last time I had seen him, he was not looking so good. My Aunt Tera, Uncle Ronald, Cousin Myia, and my grandmother greeted me, as well. It felt good to hug my grandmother again, to hear her voice and her familiar laugh. She was not the same as I remember her from my childhood. She didn't really remember me, but dementia had not taken away the smile and the laugh I remember.

I was also greeted with my favorite, down-home meal of all times... chicken and dumplings! I have loved this dish since I was a kid, and the first bite brought back so many wonderful memories. There were greens and homemade cornbread (not Jiffy...the real deal). It was the best. After dinner, I made a trip to the old snow cone stand I used to visit as a kid. I decided to try something new; blue raspberry with coconut and pineapple. It was good and brought back old memories, as well. It felt good walking through the house and seeing pictures on the wall that had been there since I was a kid. My uncle made a homemade pound cake, which topped everything off. There was some healing balm in coming "home."

That evening, my cousin took me to her apartment and we hung out for a while, looking at photos. She is my little cousin and was newly married, so it was nice to see her doing such a good job of creating her own home. I was happy for her. That night, we slept at my uncle's one-bedroom apartment and my mom and I slept in the bed together. I slept pretty well, knowing that my mother was beside me.

The next day, we headed over to my grandma's house for the day. It was my mother's sixty-third birthday and it was nice to be with her on this day. That morning, I played the song "My Testimony" by Marvin Sapp for her, and she started to cry. She said she did not understand why so many bad things were happening in her family; one brother with AIDS, one brother just free from drugs, a sister with cancer, a mother with dementia, and then me losing my baby. I tried to encourage her. We talked about how grandparents also grieve when a stillbirth occurs and can often be forgotten about, due to the focus being on the grieving parents. At my grandmother's house, I worked with my aunt and uncle to surprise my mom with a cake and ice cream. It was great to be able to celebrate her birthday as a family.

It was wonderful to have so many family members drop by to say hello. I was happy that my cousin, LaTreece, stayed for so long. She and I had grown up playing together each summer, when I visited Mississippi, and I had not seen her in a while. She looked exactly the same. LaTreece talked and talked and I just laughed. I love to laugh.

LaTreece also told me about how her middle son had recently become a father. She took out her phone to show us a picture of her adorable granddaughter, who was about two months old. I was not sure if anyone in my family had told her about my situation, but it was difficult for me to look at the pictures of the baby. I probably should have said something, but I did not want to be insensitive to her joy as a new grandmother. I am learning that just because Riley's death is at the forefront of my mind, it is not on everyone else's mind. I really do not think they are intentionally being insensitive.

Before going to Mississippi, one of my co-workers had told me to keep my ears open because God had something to speak to me through my grandmother. During our visit, my grandmother's dementia surfaced and she was upset with everybody but me. She never said anything rude and was pleasant when interacting with me. I think God's grace prevailed because He knew I was hurting. I really needed my family to love on me and that is exactly what happened. In fact, out of the blue, as I was sitting on the couch with my grandmother, she said, "I love youuuuu!" I was surprised and happy because it felt like she had finally connected with me. I thought that maybe God was telling me, through her, that He loved me.

I also gained a renewed sense of family during our visit. It blew me away how many people in my family stopped by just because I was in town, to say, "Hey!" (You know how they say it in the South.) It was as if there were no question or option; if family is in town, you go by and visit. Period! I love that. Where I live, family visits usually depend on how convenient it is for us.

LaTreece told me about her brother and sister who were not speaking to one another. She said, "I can't imagine not speaking to my brother or sisters. There is nothing that would cause me to stop speaking to them. We may disagree. I'm going to tell them how I feel and they may get upset with me, but they'll get over it. We're not going to stop talking." That really blessed me. I wanted to apply that principle to my own life; especially with my brothers and sisters in the body of Christ.

I love the value that is often placed on family in the South and how they sacrifice for one another. LaTreece also told me about a medical condition her daughter has. I had no idea about it. She said, "That's because we didn't treat it like it was what it was." When her daughter's symptoms arose, they addressed them by getting the help or treatment she needed, and then kept moving forward. That was a lesson for me; that we can overcome some things if we do not put so much focus on them.

There is such an emphasis on church and God in the South. Everyone that came over talked about needing to get home to get ready for church on Sunday. Church seemed to not be an option, but a part of life. One cousin said, "I'm not hopping from church to church. There is drama at every church so I'm going to stay right where I'm at!"

Going back to the South where my roots are was just what I needed at this point in my grieving process. I was able to spend time with those who love me and it re-connected me to my childhood summer visits, which was a time in my life that I think back on with fond memories. I was very sad to leave. I wanted to stay in this small town where life seemed simple and appeared to move at a slower pace. It felt like a safe cocoon that could protect me from anything else bad happening in my life. Although I missed my family, I did not want to return home and face my unpleasant reality.

14

Am I Losing My Mind?

Trauma has a way of bringing you to your knees. I went through a dark period in my life, a place where I had never been before and where I care never to go again. One day, while watching Joni Lamb's show, "Table Talk," Dodi Osteen was talking about her bout with cancer. Ever since God healed her, she has declared Nahum 1:9 over her life every day. It says, "...This affliction shall not come upon me a second time." Osteen has been cancer-free for thirty years now. After hearing her testimony, I took that Scripture for myself and began declaring it over my life.

This period was so horrible and so scary for me. I literally thought I was going to lose my mind and eventually die. It's something I did not even want to write about in this book because I knew I would have to re-visit it. It was a time in my life when I was afraid to go to sleep at night. I was *terrified* to go to sleep at night! I hated it when the day started to end and the sun started to go down. I would start to get sad because I knew the torment that was waiting for me. My bed was the enemy.

I've always been a person who enjoyed relaxing in bed and enjoyed sleep, but even my joys had turned against me. I really became like a crazy person and the hard part about it is that I was living in this world all alone. It was an internal world that I did not know how to escape from. I had many people praying for me and I would try my best to explain it to others, but I was so afraid that people would think I was crazy that I never told anyone everything; only bits and pieces. I had such a spirit of fear gripping me that I was even afraid to talk about it. Satan had a hold on me.

My mind was going crazy. I thought about dying almost constantly, all day. Not that I wanted to die, but I was gripped with the fear of dying and I was consumed with thoughts that I was going to. I see how people end up taking their own lives because the torment is painful and starts to feel unbearable. The only way of escape or to get some relief could seem to be to end your own life. I'm sure that is what the enemy wants; to get rid of another saint of God.

Everywhere I looked, I saw death. If I looked into the sky and saw a clear blue sky with beautiful clouds, I equated it with heaven and thought God was calling me home. Something that I used to marvel at and thank God for, its beauty now frightened me. It seemed like every television commercial or television show was talking about cancer or honoring someone who passed away. I just knew that I was going to get cancer and die. The scary thing was, no one knew that all of this was going on in my mind.

I was desperate at night and tried anything to stay up or to get restful sleep. My oldest daughter is a late-night worker, so I would get so excited if I woke up at 2:00 or 3:00 a.m. from a horrible nightmare and saw her light on. I would go in the room with her and read or use my computer. I became obsessed with reading up on health issues. I needed to figure out a way to stay healthy so that I could beat this death that seemingly was chasing me down.

One night, I decided to sleep downstairs on the couch because I could leave the light and the television on all night and it would not bother anyone. My daughter stayed downstairs on the computer, working on a website until four o'clock the next morning. I was so excited because I was not alone. By the time she left for work, it was almost morning.

I craved daylight. I was so happy when the sun rose each day because I could finally go to sleep. I was exhausted each morning and I felt like I had been fighting all night. I woke up, helped to get my younger daughter ready for school, got back in the bed, turned on the television to watch Joyce Meyer or Kenneth Copeland, and finally drifted off to sleep until around 11:00 a.m. Then I could get up and start my day. I became upset when my husband wanted to go to bed at night, because that meant the lights had to go out and my fight with the dark spiritual world would begin.

In order to keep myself sane, I purchased a few sets of teaching CDs from Kenneth and Gloria Copeland and Joyce Meyer on the topics of faith and fear. They also taught on being mindful of the words you speak because they have the power to bring things to pass in your life. I listened to these teachings over and over again, everywhere I went. I even loaded them on my phone so that I could listen to them at night while I slept. I let the Word play over and over again in my ears so that I could be protected while I slept.

I also purchased some CDs on healing and made a music playlist titled *Healing 2012*, which I listened to constantly. I was holding on to these things for dear life. I had horrible nightmares, and since God had spoken to me prophetically through dreams in the past, I wondered if He was telling me that I was going to die. I really believe the enemy distorted my thinking during this period, causing me to think my dreams were from God when, in reality, they were not.

I had dreams that I was going to die by stepping off a plane into the sky; that people were out to kill me; and that people were asking me, "How does it feel to only have three months to live?" It was crazy making! One night, I woke up and had a panic attack. I thought that if I could just stay up, I could preserve my life. I was afraid of my kids being without a mother and my husband being sad about losing me, having to parent alone, and even eventually remarry. Each day, I hugged my kids for a long time because I really did not know how much time we had. I mean, who was to say that God would not take one of us like He took Riley?

I felt safe around people. On the night that I had the panic attack, I woke Greg up and asked him to read some Scriptures with me. I remembered Kenneth Copeland saying that when he had severe pain in his leg, his wife Gloria sat in bed and read Scriptures to him. So, I thought it was worth a try. I was desperate. I would try anything! Greg found Scripture after Scripture on fear and I read them out loud. It was a blessing. I was so happy that he actually helped me instead of getting mad or thinking I was crazy.

I had never had a panic attack before. My heart was beating so fast and would not slow down. My breathing was shallow and I was really hot. Eventually, I called my mom in Georgia. She said that when that happens to her, she has to change her scenery/environment by going to a cooler, dimly lit room. So, I left my bedroom and sat on the leather couch in the loft, where it was cool. I immediately calmed down and my heart rate slowed. Whew! Thank you, Jesus. That was scary.

During this season in my life, I was hyper focused on all of the young people who had seemed to die too soon. Music artist Marvin Sapp's wife was forty-two years old, the same age as me, when she died of cancer. A co-worker's daughter was twenty-three years old and died of cancer within three months of her diagnosis. These were women who had loved God and served Him and He still took their lives. I could not understand. They had left children and husbands behind. When I thought about these premature deaths, God seemed cruel to me. I started to get scared because I wanted to live a long, full life with my family. I wanted to see my kids grow up and get married, to become a grandma, and to watch my grandchildren live full lives. I just wasn't sure anymore if this was going to happen for me. I began to covet people who lived to an old age.

One day, I was in the mall and saw a man with white hair and I thought, "Wow, you do not know how lucky you are to have lived a long life and still be here." I even began wondering what he had done to still be here. What was the secret? It just seemed so unpredictable, so random, like there was no rhyme or reason. You never knew who was next, and that freaked me out. Why did some get healed and others did not? This battle for my mind led me to buy Joyce Meyer's book, *Battlefield of the Mind*. I also bought *The Bondage Breaker* by Neil Anderson and Beth Moore's book, *Praying God's Word*. I read one chapter every morning from the Meyer and Moore books, ritually. Nothing came before that because I felt like my life depended on it.

I also was blessed by a CD by Cheryl Salem called *Why Ask Why?* I could really sense God speaking to me through all of these books, tapes, CDs, and shows, but I still could not seem to get free. I really feel like I may have been going through post-partum psychosis, which is a rare illness with symptoms such as: delusions/strange beliefs, hallucinations, irritability, hyperactivity, decreased need for or inability to sleep, paranoia/suspiciousness, rapid mood swings, and difficulty communicating at times. A woman experiencing psychosis is experiencing a break from reality. In her psychotic state, the delusions and beliefs make sense to her; they feel very real to her and are often religious in nature. Although I was never professionally diagnosed, I began to empathize with the women we hear about in the news who have harmed their precious children due to being in an altered mental state.

The sleep deprivation made me feel like I was losing my mind. I got delirious and my thoughts became more and more irrational. I thank God for preserving my life during this season. I'm thankful that I did not do anything to harm myself or anyone else. I resorted to drinking. I could see then why some resort to alcohol, prescription medication, cutting, suicide, homicide, promiscuity, and the whole gamut. I would do almost anything to bring relief.

I praise God for anti-depressants. I really believe that they saved my life. I was becoming more and more unraveled. I resisted the little blue pill, but eventually I was grateful for it. I could sleep, enjoy my bed, and watch television again. God is good.

This experience showed me how important it is to not let pride, stigmas, or stereotypes get in the way of getting help. God used a therapist, a psychiatrist, and a little blue pill to give me back my life, my joy, and my peace. My quality of life was restored.

15

Going Back to Work

As the time drew closer and closer for me to return to my work at the local homeless shelter, I began looking forward to it so that I could have something to do. Going back to work would give me some type of routine. So many people had mentioned that having a routine would help me feel better faster, so I bought into that idea. Maybe it works well for some people, but going back to work proved to be very hard for me.

My first day went very well. I put on a new outfit that I had purchased when my friend Felicia and I were out shopping. I looked and felt very cute. My hair and makeup were done. My boss said that I could come in at 10:30 a.m. that day, to meet with her and the director of the new program. That was just fine with me because I had not woken up early for work in months. This would give me the opportunity to ease back into things.

As soon as I pulled up in front of the building, the first person I saw was a co-worker whose wife was due to deliver their baby on the same day that Riley had been due. I made sure not to make eye contact with him and just kept driving. As I pulled into the parking garage, I hoped not to see anyone who would ask me any questions. I decided not to go in through the normal entrance because I did not want to see any of the clients from the program I directed prior to my medical leave. Nor did I want to see any of my staff. I definitely did not want to be around any babies. So, I chose to walk all the way around the building to enter through the front main entrance.

I was so happy not to see anyone in the elevator. When I got to the sixth floor, I only saw one person before making it into my boss' office. She just said, "Hello, good to have you back." That was easy. Whew! My supervisor and I sat down with the director of the program to which I was temporarily transferring, to discuss how my new position would look. I previously was director of a women and children's recovery program, which involved working with many babies and toddlers. I was not ready to see women with babies on a daily basis yet, so I asked my supervisor if I could temporarily transfer to another available position within the organization. I was grateful that she approved my request.

As we began to discuss the position, neither of them was clear on what they wanted this position to look like. I left feeling uncertain about what my actual job would be. This was hard for me because I really like things to be clear and thought-out. In the end, it was left up to me and the other director to clarify the position. It did not go well.

My new office was much smaller than the office I had left in the Women's Center. It was not yet set up for me. The space was dirty, unorganized, had wires traveling across the floor, and there were no office supplies in place. I could not help feeling like my employer had not taken the time to prepare for my return. This unfulfilled expectation was hard for me to deal with.

I spent most of my first days back trying to come up with a plan to get my office organized and livable. I thought that if I could just get my office looking nice, I could feel better. I contacted the administrative assistant in my old department and asked if she could get some of my personal items out of my former office so that I could use them to decorate my new, temporary space. That definitely helped a little. I also spent time reading through emails and cleaning up old emails that had been there since I left, a couple of months prior. It was nice having a little time to focus on some things I am usually too busy for, like organizing my therapy files, calculating my hours toward licensure, and re-doing my experience verification forms.

I tried to figure out what was wrong with me, because whenever I met with Program Director, I always felt like crying. I think the fact that he was not clear about what he needed from me, that I felt like they had not prepared for my return, the loss of my staff, and my new, tiny box of an office were just too much for me. I had to work very hard to keep it together whenever he came to meet with me.

I had done a good job of avoiding people from my old department because they had been through the pregnancy with me and would want to talk about it. But one day, I went upstairs to use the restroom and I ran into both the guy who took over my position and another fellow therapist. The therapist gave me a hug and asked how I was doing. It was hard for me to look at my replacement. He was very sympathetic and I could feel the hurt in his eyes. I knew that he and his wife had welcomed a baby just a couple of months before Riley was delivered. It was hard for me, knowing they were enjoying their baby and that I did not have mine. As soon as our conversation ended, I went downstairs and grabbed my things to head home.

My boss had told me to leave early if I needed to, and this day, I was about to fall apart. I made it into the parking garage before I started crumbling, as I walked to my car. As soon as I closed the car door, I let it all out. I hoped that no one would stop me and want to talk as I drove out. I cried all the way home. I headed to my youngest daughter's school, parked the car, and sat there for who knows how long, crying. I kept trying to get myself together so that I could pick her up from after-school care, but I could not walk in there with my face all red. Eventually, I drove across the street to pick up my middle daughter from school first, so that she could go in and get Noelle for me.

On another day, I went into the copier room on the sixth floor. One of my co-workers from my old department was making copies and

I could tell she was uncomfortable around me. She said a few words and then ran out of the room without her copies. She said she would get them later. I felt like I had the plague. I wanted people to act normal and not ask me any questions, but I also did not want them to act like nothing had happened. I did not know what I wanted, so how could they possibly know how to act around me? It was a weird space to be in.

A co-therapist, with whom I had worked with prior to my leave of absence, scheduled a follow-up family therapy session for us, with a client that we had been seeing together. He had not met with them since I left, and this was to be his first session seeing them again. He invited me to the session, but I was not up to seeing clients yet, so I declined. I still needed to get my emotions under control. As I was leaving the building, however, I saw the family in the lobby, as they were waiting for the therapist. I did not want to see them and deal with the question of, "How is the baby?"

I had met with this family throughout my entire pregnancy. Their daughter was now five months old and they usually brought her to our therapy sessions. She was adorable. Before Riley's arrival, I had frequently asked to hold her, to get into the habit of holding babies again, since I would soon be holding my own little girl.

The therapist graciously retrieved the family from the lobby and escorted them around the building one way, while I walked around the building in the opposite direction to the parking garage where my car was located. I felt like a secret spy, sneaking around like that. I felt like my grief was controlling me and making me do crazy things. I decided that I needed to start facing it and answering people's questions. I could not avoid it any longer.

I asked the human resources director if she could send out an email to the staff, letting them know that this topic was still sensitive for me and that I would appreciate it if they would not ask me questions about my situation. I hoped that sending the email would help, but actually it made it more awkward.

In the midst of all of this, my husband realized that I was slipping into a black hole that he could not pull me out of. Out of love and concern, he scheduled an appointment with our therapist. During the session, I made a statement that brought a sense of urgency to her concern for me. I stated, "It's all just too much!" She asked, "Nikki, what is too much?" "Everything!" I stated.

At that point, she recommended that I get connected with my psychiatrist immediately. In her professional opinion, I needed to be taken off work again for a period of time. Upon her recommendation and in conjunction with the psychiatrist's evaluation, I was removed from my job for another three months. I was completely relieved. I needed more time to adjust to my new normal.

16

The Beach

Without the routine of a job to go to each day, I needed something to occupy my time and get me out of the house. I felt like the walls were closing in on me. One day, my mom suggested going to the beach. We went to Panera Bread first, to purchase some sandwiches to take with us to eat for lunch. We drove out to Coronado and decided to take the scenic route through Imperial Beach.

We parked down the street from the Hotel Del Coronado, on a little side street near the beach. As we exited the car, there was a guy making beautiful designs in the parking lot, with sand and a push broom. After grabbing our blanket and lunches, we found a nice spot to set up camp. We sat out there for hours and I wrote the beginnings of this book while my mom worked on the edits for the second edition of her first book. Diamond was supposed to be reading; however I think she slept most of the time.

Not long after we started eating our lunch, birds suddenly surrounded us! It was as if someone had told them there was food available. It was weird, how they knew that the food was out. Diamond was our bird chaser. Whenever they got too close, she chased them away. It was kind of funny.

My mom eventually returned to her home in Georgia, and my daughter and I continued going to the beach each week. Sitting out by the water was very comforting and peaceful for me. It was my way of escape. I love water. It is very relaxing for me to sit and look at it and I believe that it is one of God's greatest creations and that it has healing power.

On one of our weekly visits, Diamond and I took the Coronado Bridge to the beach because I wanted a different view. We parked and, like always, we saw the guy who draws in the sand. With the national election happening then, he had made sand drawings of the White House and tributes to Obama. We laid our blanket out and relaxed while I wrote.

I took a nice long stroll down to the Hotel Del Coronado. On my way back, I strolled along the beach and started to see shells. I knew that one of my friends had a birthday coming up and she loved shells, so I decided to collect them for her as birthday a gift. It is very rare to find many whole seashells, but on this day, I felt like God had me find a lot of them, just for her. It was therapeutic for me to just walk along the water looking for shells, and I got excited every time I added a new shell to my collection. I was happy, thinking about how much she would be blessed by the gift that money cannot buy.

I not only found a variety of beautiful, whole shells (black, white, brown, orange, clam, oyster, hermit crab, etc.), but I also found a whole sand dollar (which I knew she would love). As I was walking, I looked ahead and saw a huge clamshell that was the size of my hand! I started walking fast because I did not want anyone else to get it and I did not want the water to wash it away. There was a group of people standing near it, so I just knew it belonged to them. As I approached it and bent down to pick it up, I thought they would tell me it belonged to them. But they kept walking and I was in absolute awe at the size of the shell. It was huge, heavy, and WHOLE! I was so excited. I felt like God had placed that shell in my path just for my friend. I could not wait to get back to

Diamond to show her my finds. It was so nice to have something to get excited about again.

Initially I thought the whole shells I was finding were just for my friend. But looking back, I believe God placed those whole shells in my path that day to communicate to me that I would one day find wholeness again. The joy I felt at finding those shells was merely a foreshadowing of the joy I would one day experience again.

As we left, we stopped to talk to the sand artist and he told us the story of how he had gotten started. After this visit, the weather began to get cooler, so we no longer went to the beach.

17

Down's Syndrome

On November 8, 2012, I received a phone call from the gynecologist that followed me throughout the pregnancy. She called to say that she had received the results from the genetic testing to determine the cause of Riley's death. Prior to receiving the call, I wondered if I would be able to receive the news or if Greg should handle it. I feared that Riley's condition was the result of something genetically wrong with me.

We learned that Riley had Down's Syndrome, which is also known as Trisomy 21. The doctor explained the heart problems associated with the condition and the higher incidence of stillbirth in babies affected by it. She mentioned that if we had done an amniocentesis, we would have known about the Down's Syndrome earlier.

Riley's diagnosis also explained some of the features that I had wondered about. She had some extra skin at the nape of her neck, her head was a little misshapen, and her nose was a bit flattened. I went online to find out more about Down's Syndrome and found out that skin at the nape of the neck is common. Down's babies tend to have smaller ears, a wide gap between the first and second toe, shortened femur bones, etc. The condition is called Trisomy 21 because during conception, the babies end up with an extra twenty-first chromosome. Each person has twenty-three chromosomes and we generally receive two of each; one from each parent. But in the case of Trisomy 21, the baby receives two from the mother and one from the father. Nothing that can be done to prevent this anomaly; it just happens.

I felt a lot better, knowing for sure that nothing I had done had caused Riley's Down's Syndrome. I still wondered to myself if, having been so sick in the first trimester that I did not eat well, if I had provided the nutrition that Riley needed. I had feared that maybe it had been the fact that I found out too late about my extremely low iron levels. Iron is responsible for carrying oxygen in the blood, so I thought that maybe she had not gotten enough oxygen because of me. Maybe the pills I took for morning sickness had caused the Down's Syndrome, even though the doctors said they were harmless. All of these thoughts still went through my mind. Now I am able to have some level of peace, knowing that this chromosome abnormality was not preventable on my part.

As I read about Down's Syndrome, I found out that many babies born with this condition end up having heart surgery shortly after birth. Many more end up needing gastrointestinal surgery, as well. It would have been so hard to handle having a little baby with so many surgeries.

We had opted not to have the amniocentesis or any other testing during the pregnancy because our thinking was that if anything were wrong with Riley, we would not abort her, so what difference would it make? But now, looking back, I probably would have done it because at least we would have been mentally prepared for her condition. But who knows? We probably would have spent a lot of time researching Down's Syndrome and preparing for it and not enjoyed the pregnancy. Had she survived, I think we would have been totally shocked to find out that she had Down's Syndrome.

God had instructed us to get pregnant and it just seemed baffling that He would tell us to do something that would not bear fruit in the normal way. What was the purpose? We know there is one. God is not cruel, so we have to also believe that there is a good purpose. Maybe Riley needed to be born so that I could write this book to help others make it through the process. Maybe she had to be born to bring me and my husband, and ultimately, our family closer. I do not know. After listening to a teaching by Pastor Kenneth Copeland, I realized that if we have surrendered our will to God and His will becomes our will, then our only responsibility is to do His will. We had done that. If this outcome was His will, then we would have to choose to be okay with that because we trust that His will is only good for us; not good according to our human standards, but according to God's standards, which means it is for our highest good. According to Isaiah 55:9, "As the heavens are higher than the earth, so are my ways higher than your ways and my thoughts than your thoughts."

A friend of my spiritual mom suggested that we should find out why Riley was *born*, as opposed to why she had to *die*. Profound! Greg and I began to focus on that idea. I was also reminded of something Pastor Charles Stanley said on his radio program, *Insights for Living*: "Obey God and leave the consequences to Him." We did just that; we obeyed God. That was our only responsibility. And we have decided to leave the consequences to Him.

18

The Cruise

Greg was adamant that we needed to take a trip together as a family, to get away from what we were dealing with. He did all the work, booking the cruise and putting together a manual of all of the possible excursions. On December 2, 2013, we headed to the airport to take a red-eye flight to Port Canaveral, Florida, from where the cruise ship would depart.

At the airport on the night of our flight, as we went to purchase our dinner, we saw a little girl with Down's Syndrome. Although I still struggled with sadness at the sight of her, I prayed for her and her family, understanding in a new way the struggles they must live with. I never would have done this before, as Down's Syndrome was not on my radar. I have learned that some things in the world can be invisible to us until we have to deal with them in our own lives. Not only did we see this little girl at the airport, but guess what? She was on our plane in the row right behind us. Of all of the planes in the airport and then of all the seats on the airplane, what are the odds?

Our plane landed at 5:45 a.m. and we had breakfast in the Hilton hotel attached to the airport. The doors opened at 6:30 a.m. and we were the first ones there, with luggage and all. We enjoyed a beautiful view from of the sun rising. As we ate our breakfast, we took our time because our ground transportation would not arrive until 9:45 a.m. We stayed in the restaurant for as long as we could, and then headed out to the hotel. We found an area with a couple of benches and decided to camp out for a while to relax, and wait for our ride.

Finally, we headed downstairs to meet our ground transportation. Greg had wanted to surprise us and he had a driver pick us up. He was determined that everything on our trip would be perfect and just as he planned. He really wanted to spoil us.

We all piled into the van and I have to admit it was nice and plush. It was very roomy with plush leather seats, Wi-Fi, a television and a DVD player, with several DVDs for us to choose from. We chose a movie for the kids to watch. I watched it off and on during the ride and I was on my laptop at other times, watching a movie I had brought with me.

Greg sat up front and talked with the driver during the whole forty-five minutes of the trip. Once we arrived at the dock, workers took our bags and loaded them on the ship. I was so tired that night because I had not been able to sleep on the plane and had been up pretty much for over twenty-four hours. I was starting to feel delirious, so I went in our room to take a nap for a while. I fell right into a deep sleep.

Later that evening, we all played a few games of Uno. It was Noelle's first time playing, and she loved it. The next morning, we all got off the ship and spent a fun-filled day in Nassau, Bahamas. The kids had so much fun shopping at the little stores and buying souvenirs with their money. The younger ones made sure to buy gifts for friends.

We also made our way to a beautiful beach with clear water and white sand. We rented beach chairs and Greg and I lay out while the girls splashed in the water for hours. It was so fun to see the girls playing together and laughing again. Joy. We had not laughed in a while.

Natives walked the beach selling sarongs, jewelry, and musical instruments. The girls wanted to buy sarongs and they convinced me to get one, as well. Greg took lots of pictures. Finally, after getting back on the ship, we took a tour to view all of the amazing amenities available for us to enjoy. There was so much to see, including an ice skating rink, a rock climbing wall, a surf simulator, and so much more! It was a lot to take in and we all wanted to do and see everything.

At one point, the girls and I took a trip to the library while Greg was in the golf simulator. We all love to read, so we were excited to see what we could find. I helped to find books for both Noelle and Sydney, and then took a look around for myself. I looked at all of the sections with adult books and came up empty handed. Some things looked interesting, but during this period, I only wanted to read books that would help me feel better. So I sat down with Noelle, to look through her books. Diamond said, "Mom, did you see this book?" I walked over to her and my mouth dropped open. She wondered what was wrong. I could not believe my eyes. The book she was holding was in a section of the library where I had spent the most time browsing and had somehow overlooked.

I'm convinced that God had put *When I Lay My Isaac Down* by Carol Kent (Navpress, 2004) there just for me. Just two weeks earlier, I had been watching the Joni Lamb show for the first time and Kent was the guest, talking about this book! I had never heard of the author before, but her story of grief over her only child being sentenced to life in jail for murdering his wife's ex-husband intrigued me. After the show was over, I had added her book to my list of titles to buy, and now Diamond was holding it. If this had happened a month prior, I would have probably looked at the book and passed it up because I would have had no clue who Kent was. God was still showing me how much He cared for me, all the way in the middle of the ocean on a cruise ship.

I checked the book out and took it everywhere I went on the cruise ship. I read it on the balcony when I woke up, in bed before I went to sleep, on the deck while lying out relaxing, and on the beach in the Virgin Islands. I ate it up. I could identify with Kent. She could feel my pain. It was amazingly healing. I was sad when I did not finish the story before we left the ship. I felt like I had to put my friend back on the shelf, but as soon as I got home, I purchased it for my Kindle and finished it. God is good. I purchased her next book, *Between a Rock and a Grace Place* (Zondervan, 2013), which also blessed me. Other books that encouraged me on this journey are *Love, Mom: A Mother's Journey from Loss to Hope* by Cynthia Baseman (AuthorHouse, 2006), *A Thousand Gifts* by Ann Voskamp (Zondervan, 2011), *The Bondage Breaker* by Neil Anderson (Harvest House, 2006), and *I Will Carry You* by Angie Smith (B & H Books, 2013).

One of our favorite parts of the cruise was the food! It was so nice to have "free" food at our disposal. We ate and ate and ate. We rarely gave ourselves the opportunity to get hungry. There was the Windjammer Café, which served hot dogs, hamburgers, sandwiches, pasta, chicken smothered in a variety of sauces, and lots of tasty desserts. There was the pizza parlor with ready-made pizza, Panini's, and salads. The bakery had cookies, cakes, and mini sandwiches available all day. The self-serve soft ice cream machine was available on the deck twenty-four hours a day.

But our favorite place to eat was at the dining hall every evening. Our waitress' name was Sophia and she became our friend for the week. She knew our names and she even learned our likes and dislikes. The kids looked forward to seeing her each evening. We had two formal nights where we all dressed up fancy. That was fun. We rarely all get dressed up together as a family. On lobster night, which Diamond looked forward to all week long, she ate two-and-a-half lobster tails. It was all you can eat and she would have eaten more if I had not convinced her that she would probably get sick. It was nice to have breakfast, lunch, dinner, and desserts all taken care of. We did not have to worry about a budget or figuring out where to eat to please everyone. There was something for everyone, and we could eat our heart's fill.

It was such a nice, pampering experience. We did not even have to make up our beds. Our cabin attendant, Rhonda, came in daily and made our beds, picked up our room and bathroom, and provided new towels. To top it off, she always left an animal towel creation on our beds each evening while we were at dinner. One of the highlights of the kids' trip was getting back to the room each evening after dinner, to see what new creation they would find.

One evening, while she was leaving the room, I heard her singing, "Oh, how I love Jesus. Oh, how I love Jeee-suuus. Oh, how I love Jesus because He first loved me." I was blown away. In the middle of the ocean in the Virgin Islands, a cruise staff member from another country was singing about Jesus while folding towels in the hallway. It was proof to me that God is everywhere!

When I made a comment about her singing that song, she said, "He loves me, girl!" I loved it! All I could say was, "Amen!" We hear so many stories about how cruise ship crew members work long hours, sleep in cramped quarters, earn low wages, and usually take the job to escape their own poverty and see the world. In the midst of all of that, Rhonda was singing about the love of God. It was amazing and humbling.

We went on excursions in St. Thomas and St. Marten, as well. In St. Thomas, we booked an excursion through Royal Caribbean. We were loaded onto a big red tour bus with a lot of other families. It was fun getting to know some of the other people from various parts of the United States.

Once we arrived at the beach in St. Thomas, Greg and the girls snorkeled while I searched for seashells in the sand. Each time the water rolled back, I tried to grab the exposed seashells before the water made its way back to shore. This was fun and relaxing. The seashells were tiny oyster shells that were actually still closed. I was so excited to gather as many as I could, and found about thirty of them. I wanted to take them home to my seashell-loving friend because I knew she loved them. Greg was convinced they would stink up the room, but that never happened.

While on the island of St. Marten, we went to the beach where the planes fly low overhead. Greg took tons of pictures. This was one of the highlights of his trip. I have to admit that it was pretty cool. Once back on the ship, Greg and I celebrated Greg's fortieth birthday by going on a date to the steakhouse onboard. We had a great time, a beautiful view, and a great waiter. The food was amazing! They even surprised Greg by bringing him a plate that was festively decorated in chocolate and spelled out "Happy Birthday."

While we were out to dinner, I paid the cruise staff to decorate our cabin and deliver a birthday cake so that Greg could be surprised when he returned. Greg was surprised and left the decorations up for the rest of the trip. I was happy that I could bring him some semblance of joy.

One day, we went shopping in the center of the ship, where I created and bought my "R-i-l-e-y" bracelet at a beading shop. I had wanted to get a keepsake and when I saw this opportunity, I knew it was perfect. I wore the bracelet almost every day for many months after the cruise.

Greg and I also took some time alone. As we sat there relaxing, I marveled at how pampered we had been all week. I told Greg that I felt like God wanted to pamper us after all of the pain we had been through.

There were many times during the cruise when Greg was testy, overly sensitive, and easily frustrated. I tried to give him some space because I knew what it was most likely stemming from. He was dealing with depression as a result of missing Riley. We all knew that the purpose of the trip was to give us some joy in our lives after living through something so traumatic. Even though it was fun and relaxing, there was this underlying *knowing* of why we were there. Had Riley never passed and been home and healthy, we would never have been on that cruise because we would have been home caring for her.

This trip was a wonderful blessing for our family. It gave us the opportunity to get away from home and the constant reminder of our loss. It was an escape from the pain we left at home and gave us an opportunity to be a joyful family again. This vacation will always be a special memory for us.

Part Three

A New Normal

19

Back to "Normal" Again

few weeks after returning from the family cruise, I began to get really sad because I realized that I only had one more week with Diamond before she would return to college. At times, tears spilled out of my eyes uncontrollably. She had re-assessed her situation, changed her major, and spent countless hours researching which one had the best program for her major.

Where had the time gone? I had gone from being frustrated that she was coming home early from college to being sad that she was leaving because I had gotten used to having her around. We had so much fun together.

On the day that Diamond was to leave for college, both Greg and I were very sad. The weather outside matched our mood, as it was cloudy, dreary, and raining heavily. When we got to the train station, we boarded the train with Diamond so that Greg could load her luggage. After we got her settled, it was time to say good-bye. Greg gave her a hug first and then it was my turn. I tried to hold back the tears, but I could not. My oldest baby was leaving me. I felt like I was losing a child again.

I did not want her to feel sad, but I could not hold it in. I told her to not worry about me, to just go and do what she needed to do because she has a big purpose in this world. I was very surprised to look over and see Greg crying, too. As we got off the train and headed back to our truck, I continued to cry. The rain began falling harder and it seemed like the sky was crying along with me.

A month later I finally returned back to work for the second time. Although I did not quite feel ready to return, my psychiatrist determined that I was emotionally well enough to do so. I was released to return, working half days for the first month to ease back into working into a residential program where young children would be present.

When I went into the break room on the first day back, the custodian was in there and greeted me with, "Long time no see!" We exchanged pleasantries and then he asked THE question; the one I thought everyone in the world should already know the answer to: "Did you have the baby?" Once again, I was caught off guard. I kind of fumbled my way through my answer that my baby was born stillborn. I had a hard time being prepared with a smooth reply. Of course, he apologized and it was awkward for a few seconds before he started talking about other things to fill the pause that always seems to be filled with "I'm so sorry I asked."

Later that day, my colleague, Mary, came into my office and closed the door behind her. She said, "Finally, I get to talk to you by myself." She had waited for thirty-five minutes after her shift had ended, just to say hello to me and give me a hug. I thought that her gesture was really sweet, but I did not realize that there was more to it.

She told me that she had been fasting for me, hoping that I would come back to work. She showed me where she had marked "Fasting MSN" on her wall calendar each day over the past month. The acronym stood for "Fasting for Ms. Nikki." She said that my return to work was a sign for her that God does hear and answer her prayers. I gave her a big hug and thanked her. I know how much of a sacrifice fasting is, even when you are fasting for your own needs.

She was quick to tell me to thank God and not her because she just was being obedient. Wow, what humility! She did not want credit. I thanked the Lord for showing me that He has people interceding for me when I do not even know it. He is still mindful of me. A few minutes after this interaction, words to the song *I Understand* by Smokey Norful came to mind: "I am the Lord, I hear you, and yes, I understand!" Wow! Praise God. He is so good. The second time around it was much easier to return to work. I was emotionally in a better place and my team was very sensitive to my needs. I finally felt like I was entering the land of the living again; one small step at a time.

20

Divine Intervention

Seven months after Riley went to Heaven, my spiritual mother, Donna, invited me to a women's conference. She paid for all of her daughters (natural and spiritual) to attend this conference with her. I was excited to be invited and looked forward to getting spiritually fed. I went expecting God to show up for me because I was so low and felt depleted. When the day of the conference came, I was not in a good place emotionally. I was just not in a good mood. I was a bit irritable and sad about Riley. I'm not sure why I had a wave of grief on this particular day, but it would not let up. Donna had invited me to ride with her, but I would have to be at her house by 7:30 a.m. and I could not get myself together that early, so I met her at the conference instead.

I really enjoyed listening to the conference speakers. They were very transparent about their hurts and pains and how God had carried them through rough periods. They also talked about how God had transformed their lives.

The conference was to end around 5:00 p.m., but at about 2:00 p.m., everyone at my table decided that they needed to leave. It seemed that there was nothing else for me to do but go home and be sad, so I figured that I might as well stay and get more teaching from the Word. Maybe God still had something left for me. I wanted make sure that I did not miss anything.

As I sat at the table, I jotted down: *I have no clue what to do. I feel so lonely and empty sometimes. I feel like I don't know what to do with my emotions. I'm sure everyone is tired of hearing about this. What do you say? Riley, I miss you. I really like your name. I'm so sad that I'll never be able to call your name…to kiss you…to smell your neck.*

I sat through the last speaker's message, which was good, but I still did not feel like I knew why God had me at this conference. I did not receive a sure word for myself. As the program ended, the organizers gave some closing words mentioned that this was not just a conference, but a ministry, as well. She wanted to make sure that no one left without receiving prayer, if they wanted it. She invited anyone to raise their hands if they wanted prayer. I was so sad and broken that I definitely needed prayer. I needed *everything* God had for me.

As I raised my hand, I completely trusted God to select whom He wanted to pray for me. Usually, I try to pick out who I think would be the best person to pray for me, but I realized this time that I needed to surrender complete control of my life to God and let Him have His way completely. A woman named Gwen came over, to pray for me. She had visited our table earlier in the day to talk with Donna, because they were friends.

As soon as Gwen started praying for me, I broke down. I cried like a baby! I could not contain it. I just laid on her and cried. I needed a release from the pain. As she prayed for me, Gwen said that she was sure God still had a purpose for me in this situation. She said that her niece had lost a baby girl, too. She later opened a business and named it after her daughter. She also eventually had another baby. I really believe that when I heard Gwen's story, God planted a seed in me to name the residential housing facility I planned to open in the future after Riley. One day, I will have a Riley's House.

Gwen was amazing! She was a Godsend. After she finished praying for me, she gave me her number and told me to call her any time, if I needed someone to talk to. She did not know me at all, but she extended herself to continue to be there for me during this difficult time in my life. I pray that God pours blessings on her for this selfless action. God is truly amazing. This is how the body of Christ is supposed to work.

Gwen suggested that I attend a Griefshare™ group at a local church. My Spiritual Mother, Donna, led the support group and I remembered when she first purchased the curriculum years ago. She was so excited to bring it to her church. At the time, I had no clue that I would need it one day. Even though I knew about Griefshare, pride kept me from joining the group. I thought I could battle this grief thing on my own. I was not going to take medication and I was not going to a support group; or so I thought.

That night, I sent Donna a message, to ask about the group. She responded that she had a group in session at the time and I was welcome to join. She also told me that she knew God sent me to the group because the next meeting's topic was the loss of a child. God's timing is always so amazing and His love is so great for us, even when we resist Him.

I joined the Griefshare group the following Tuesday and went nearly every week until the series ended. It was the key to my healing. The group was a safe place for me to talk about my pain with others who could identify with the pain of grief and loss.

After the first session, Donna told me that attending the group was good, but if I wanted true healing I would need to invest the time and money into the workbook *Your Journey from Mourning to Joy* (Griefshare, 2012) because it was filled with God's Word, which is the only true source of healing. I chose to believe her. I paid the $15 for the workbook and committed to do the weekly homework.

It was not an easy process. Each week, I was challenged to face the hard reality of what I was really feeling inside regarding my loss. I read Scriptures and answered questions that made me dig deep into those places where I had not allowed myself to go. There was not one corner of my soul left untouched.

Although at first I did not want to read the book or answer the questions, the more I did, the freer I became. I could no longer hide my feelings. Everything was exposed on the pages of this workbook and it was through it that the real healing work took place.

Here are two of my journal writings from it:

April 15, 2013 — The most important thing for me to focus my time and energy on is being emotionally available for my family, especially my kids. Even if they have needs that are not grief related, I still need to provide them with a safe place to share how they are feeling. I need to continue to share my emotions with my husband so that he will know that I'm still grieving, too...to taking time to relax when I need to...to allow my family to see me grieve. I don't have the emotional resources to be there for friends. I need to stay in therapy, stay connected with God, and follow His voice. I need to let myself off the hook when I feel overwhelmed and allow others, especially my husband, to help me.

April 23, 2013 — I am really not sure why God doesn't answer all of my questions. I'm guessing that it's because He knows I'm not able to handle all of the answers. I am limited in my humanity to be able to understand the deep things of God. Since He is a good God, He knows it's best not to give me all of the answers. He doesn't have to answer my questions. It's hard because, of course, I want a logical reason as to why this happened. But I'm really not sure that God's answer would justify what happened; and that would not be a good place to be with Him. I know He is good, loving, caring, compassionate, holy, righteous, long-suffering, merciful, and full of grace. He longs to bless us. He sent His Son that we might have abundant life and enjoy it. He sacrificed for us. He is all knowing, all-powerful, sovereign, wise, wonderful, just, and fair.

In His unfailing love, God continues to show His grace toward us, even when we turn our back on Him. He cared enough about my healing that He prompted my spiritual mother invite me to a conference where a lady I had never met before would pray for and minister to me. This is how the body of Christ is supposed to work. We don't have to know one another to be able to pray for one another and provide encouragement. This day was another turning point in my grief journey because it pointed me to Griefshare, where much of my healing took place.

21

Therapy

Grief is more of a journey than a destination. It is a long walk to a new way of life; a new normal. There will be good days and bad days. Some days, there may be a glimmer of hope on the horizon and other days, the sky seems gray with no sign of the sun every returning. It is unpredictable and cannot be controlled.

There is no book or script for this experience of stillbirth and it feels lonely sometimes. It is really unknown territory. It reminds me of when God told Abraham that He would take him to a country that he knew not of. I definitely did not know of this country of grief with the loss of a child. It is cold, dark, scary, uncomfortable, murky, and far away from any country I had ever visited before.

I do not believe that we could have handled something as traumatizing as Riley's death without having a caring professional to walk us through the days, months, and years ahead. Counseling played an important role in our healing process.

Being a counselor myself, I knew the importance of getting professional help immediately after our loss. I have been in counseling for years; working through many past traumas, but none of my previous experiences had been as traumatic as this one.

Thankfully, Greg also valued the therapeutic process because he has seen the transformation it has brought about in me over the years and he had even gone a few times on his own. Some couples resist this step and can implode due to suppressed grief. Or, they may attempt to cope in unhealthy ways without the proper tools available.

We decided to make counseling a part of our journey early on in our grieving process. Very soon after Riley's passing, Greg and I went to see our counselor to share the news and to find out how to walk down this new and unfamiliar road. She was surprised, as we were, at how well we were doing during the first session. Looking back, we had so many people holding our hands up, like Aaron held up Moses' hands in the Bible. The gravity of the situation had not set in yet.

Greg and I decided to alternate weeks with the counselor, with couple's counseling and then individual sessions. After Greg returned to work, he stopped going to counseling, but I continued to go weekly. Prior to this loss, I already had struggled with depression, so this experience sent me into a deeper place, where I needed help to come out. Counseling was my safe place to let out all of my emotions without being concerned that my therapist would get tired of hearing me talk about the same thing week after week. I could pour out my endless questions about how this could have happened and I could process all of the anger I had toward God.

My counselor also encouraged me to journal and she gave me several book titles to read. Each week I would bring my journal and share my inner most thoughts, no matter how irrational they were. It gave me a safe place to look forward to going. I knew I only had to be strong for six days a week because on the seventh day, I could go to see my counselor and let down the guard I wore all week.

My therapist worked closely with my psychiatrist to monitor my progress and manage my medication intake. Week after week, I got stronger and stronger. Having a Christian counselor made all the difference for me. Not only was she able to give me technical counseling insight, but she also prayed with me and encouraged me with the Word of God. She cried with me, laughed with me, encouraged me, and challenged me. She was in the fight with me, determined to not let this tragedy take me under.

22

Riley's First Birthday

Wow, it's amazing how time keeps moving. Had it really been a year since Riley was born? It seemed like a long time ago and yet, like it was just a few months ago at the same time. Greg and I decided to take off work and asked the girls if they wanted to take off from school. Noelle immediately said she wanted to be with us for Riley's birthday, but Sydney said she did not want to miss school. School had only been in session for a couple of weeks and she remembered how behind she had gotten in her school work last year, when she missed school as a result of Riley passing away. I assured her that it would not be the same because she would only be missing one day this time, as opposed to having missed many days last year. When I explained that she would be the only one not with the family on Riley's birthday, she changed her mind.

I was excited that Diamond was coming home to be with us, as well. We had planned to connect with her via Skype on Riley's birthday so that she could be a part of the remembrance, but my mom paid for her to fly home early to be with us. That was a wonderful blessing and I was happy that we were all together.

Riley's birthday was on a Tuesday, so we all slept in a little bit, since no one had work or school. We decided that we would all be ready to start our day around 11:00 a.m. We first went to Home Depot to purchase a gate to put around Riley's grave marker. Greg had decided early on that he wanted to put a gate around her gravesite, as other families had done, so that no one would be able to walk over the area where her body was laid to rest.

We all chimed in and took a vote on what type of gate we should get, since there were so many varieties to choose from. We eventually settled on a small, white picket fence-type of gate. Next, we headed over to Party City to pick up the balloons that Diamond had purchased as a surprise. She thought it would be a good idea for each of us to have a balloon to release at Riley's gravesite. They were a beautiful, soft pink. It touched my heart that she had thought of this detail. While at the store, we allowed Noelle to pick out a windmill to put on Riley's gravesite, as she had seen them on many of the other sites in the section of the cemetery named *Babyland*.

Finally, we headed out to Glen Abby Cemetery, to see Riley and to wish her a happy birthday. The experience was really bittersweet. We wished that she were with us, but since she was not, this was the next best way for us to celebrate her birthday. It's always hard driving up the pathway to her site, because it reminds me of the day when we rode up there in a limousine, to lay her to rest. That had been a hard, hard day.

Up to that point, I still had not gone to the gravesite on my own. I'm not sure what held me back. I just chose not to go. Even a year after Riley's burial, I did not want to go alone because that would mean accepting her death as my reality.

Once we arrived, we unloaded all of the items we had brought with us: the gate we had purchased, the balloons, some rocks we had selected from our yard to line Riley's grave marker so that the grass would not grow over it, solar lights so that she could have some light at night, and a few gardening tools to place the rocks.

We were a bit bummed out once we arrived at her actual gravesite, when we discovered that the family of the baby next to Riley had put up their own gate. Since it was so close to Riley's plot, it was going to be very difficult to put up our own gate. The one we had brought with us was no longer going to work, so we would have to take it back and come up with a plan B.

The rock project was next. Greg dug a nice little groove around Riley's marker, so that the rocks could fit. We all gathered together to place the rocks. When we were done, it looked beautiful. The rocks matched her marker so well. I placed a special rock right next to the marker. I received it at the last session of my GriefShare class to symbolize my grief journey. The rock was smooth with a few jagged sides, to symbolize how the journey of grief can look.

After placing the rocks, Greg set up the solar lights at each corner of the plot and Noelle placed her windmill right in the center of the site. At one point, the windmill started spinning really fast and I told everyone this was Riley telling us, "Hello, guys!" Next, Diamond handed one balloon to each of us. It took a little time to untangle them, since the wind had been blowing, but we worked together as a team to get it done. After we each had a balloon in hand, we decided that we would say a few words before releasing them.

Greg said that I should read my Facebook post from the previous night and that he would read his post from earlier that morning. Mine read: "On this night one year ago, we found out that our little princess was born into heaven. This is such a hard night, knowing that Riley would have been one year old tomorrow. It has been a hard year and a blessed year. I miss her all the time. I miss seeing her grow, and I wonder how she would have been. We will hold her one day, in heaven. She is the first person I want to see (after God). Thank God for His keeping power over this past year. He is still faithful. Love you forever, Rileykins!"

Next, Greg cried as he read his post: "I still don't understand and never will! My heart breaks every day because I can't hold you and be the father to you that I never had. I wanted you so badly, but God wanted you more. For that I say, 'Yes and amen.' I praise God for healing me and not letting me go insane. There is purpose in pain, and Riley, you are already affecting the earth. With tears of pain and joy, I say, 'Happy birthday, baby girl! Daddy loves you.'"

I can't really remember what Diamond, Sydney, and Noelle said. I remember that one of them did not want to say anything. It was really hard for Noelle to see her dad cry, so she began to tear up. We counted to three and all released our balloons at the same time. We stood there for what seemed like an hour, just watching the balloons fly into the sky. We watched them for as long as we could. My eyesight is not as good as Greg's and the girls', so I lost sight of the balloons long before they did. Greg and Diamond told Riley that these were for her, to celebrate her birthday in heaven.

Once we left Glen Abby, we were all hungry, so we headed to a Mexican taco shop to get some food. We took the food home and ate together, before heading back out to buy the items we needed for the next part of Riley's birthday celebration. I ran to the store for some cake mix, frosting, and sprinkles for her cake. We had all taken a vote on what type of cake Riley would like. At first, Diamond mentioned a Funfetti® cake and I had totally agreed. But then, we got other votes for red velvet cake. Greg pulled it all together and said, "Let's make her a red velvet-Funfetti cake." We all loved the idea, and that settled it.

My mother-in-law came over to join us in making the cake for Riley. The baking was fun and we took a lot of pictures. The younger girls took turns blending the cake batter, Carol held the bowl, and Diamond and I poured the batter into the cake pans. While the cake was baking, the girls and I looked through Riley's keepsake box. I finally allowed myself to look at the pictures from her baby shower and from her birth. This was a really special moment for me because after Riley's birth, I was in too much pain to look at either of these sets of photos. Healing was taking place.

Diamond frosted the cake, and we each took turns putting different Funfetti-like sprinkles on the cake. It came out quite beautiful and looked like a cake we thought Riley would have liked. We wanted to have a real one-year-old birthday party, so we ate cheese pizza before cutting the cake. The cake came out delicious and eating it together was the perfect ending to the perfect day.

So many people reached out to us during this time. Co-workers let me know they were praying for us and my boss surprised me by placing flowers on my desk. One of our dear family friends stopped by to drop off flowers and cupcakes in memory of Riley. That gesture really touched my heart, and her choice of red velvet cupcakes confirmed what we thought Riley's favorite cake flavor would have been. I was very touched by how many people actually remembered Riley's birthday without me mentioning it.

Celebrating Riley's first birthday was not only a way for us to celebrate her life, but also to acknowledge that we had made it through one of the toughest seasons of our lives. Although the grieving was not over by any means, we had definitely made progress and joy was starting to return to our lives. Greg and I were stronger as a couple because we needed to cling to each other to make it through this. We also learned the value of community, as our family was encircled by old and new friends from near and far to support and encourage us on this journey.

Part Four

Stories of Loss and Hope

23

Kenneth and Desiree's Story

Kenneth and Desiree originally met in high school. Although they knew of each other, they were not close during their high school years. In 1997 they ran into each other at a nightclub and sparks started flying. They had a lot in common and genuinely had a good time together. After dating for a few years, they eventually married in 2000. That year, they welcomed the arrival of their first child together, a girl.

Just one year later, Desiree found out that she was pregnant with their second child, a boy. One day, Desiree returned home from her mother-in-law's house and noticed that she did not feel the baby moving. She was pretty far along by now and knew there was not much room for movement left in her belly, but she still felt that something was not right. She decided to eat something and drink some orange juice, which normally made the baby move. When this did not work either, Desiree felt in her spirit that something was definitely wrong.

She decided to call Kenneth, when suddenly, she felt like something had popped inside of her stomach. By the time Kenneth arrived home from work, Desiree's pains had worsened, so she called the doctor. The doctor was not concerned because Desiree had just been in for a regular pre-natal check up and she still had some time left before her due date. Desiree felt that he seemed insensitive to her situation. The doctor told her to go to the emergency room if her symptoms continued to progress.

Desiree started to experience contractions, so she and Kenneth headed to the hospital. At the hospital, the nurses tried unsuccessfully to find the baby's heartbeat. They took Desiree to the ultrasound room. She asked the nurse, "Ma'am, can you tell me what is going on with my baby? Is my baby still alive?" The nurse was not at liberty to share any information, but she started crying, which gave Desiree and Kenneth the answer they were seeking. Immediately, Desiree started crying, as well.

Kenneth sat and stared off into space. He did not attempt to console Desiree in any way and he seemed to be uncaring at the time. Since then, Desiree has learned that is how Kenneth deals with painful feelings.

Once she arrived in her hospital room, Desiree began throwing things and screaming. "It was horrific," says Desiree. "It was one horrible time in my life." She felt very alone.

The baby was delivered through cesarean section. They named him Kyle. Desiree kept picking him up. She talked to him and tried to bond with him. She could not wrap her mind around the idea of leaving the hospital without him. "He was so cute and smelled so good," said Desiree.

She vaguely remembers that other people were there at the hospital with her, holding baby Kyle, but Desiree blocked out much of what happened that day, as a defense mechanism to deal with the pain. She also remembers a social worker and a chaplain coming to her room to talk about funeral arrangements. Desiree does not remember at all the day they left the hospital to return home without their baby.

In the days following her return home, Desiree pulled out Kyle's blanket and smelled it. When she was alone and during her quiet time, she looked at the pictures from the hospital over and over again. "I was tormenting myself. I could not go on; [it was] like when you go to your baby's crib to keep checking on them; I kept picking up the pictures," she says. One day, a woman at church suggested that Desiree needed to stop looking at those pictures because she was tormenting herself. Desiree knew that this message was from God because no one knew that she had been looking at Kyle's pictures. She went home and threw the pictures away, but she never forgot her baby's face.

The same lady also prophesied that Desiree would give birth to twins one day. This time, Desiree thought the prophesy was off-base because she had decided that she would never have another child, or risk going through that pain again. She was angry with God and asked Him why the stillbirth had happened to her.

When the time came to plan the burial services for Kyle, Desiree kept stalling. Eventually, her sister helped Desiree's mother-in-law to plan the services. They picked out an all-white suit for Kyle to wear and a pearl/off-white casket for his burial. Picking out the casket finally made the whole situation real for Desiree. To this day, Desiree cannot remember the details of what happened on the day of the funeral. She only remembers going out to eat afterward.

In the days that followed the funeral, Desiree did not want to be bothered. People were supportive, to the degree that she would allow them to be. "I just remember it being too much...very overwhelming," says Desiree. At the time, she was working from home, so she was able to stay to herself.

Losing her son was so painful for Desiree that she cannot remember large chunks of this time in her life. To this day, she does not remember Kyle's birthday or the gravesite where he was buried. "It's not that it wasn't important," she says. "But my mind blocked out a lot of stuff. I try not to talk about it."

She and Kenneth decided to have tests done, to see why Kyle had died. When she went for a blood test, she found out that she was pregnant again. She immediately became full of fear and did not want to have another baby. She was not happy, but she did not want to abort the baby, either.

During this pregnancy, Desiree had to take Lovenox shots in her stomach because the doctors thought Kyle's passing was the result of oxygen depletion. During this time, she found out that she had a blood-clotting disorder. Desiree was nervous throughout the entire pregnancy and was very cautious with her movements.

In 2002, Kenneth and Desiree welcomed a healthy baby boy into the world. They named him Kayden. Two years later, Desiree found out that she was pregnant again. Just as before, she was nervous about the prospect of losing the baby. This pregnancy also was considered high-risk and Desiree was not prepared mentally or physically for all it entailed.

The first seven months of the pregnancy went well, and then one day, she started having contractions. She immediately called Kenneth. When he arrived, her water completely broke, and they both started freaking out.

Once she arrived at the hospital, Desiree delivered Kendall Smith. The hospital staff told Kenneth and Desiree that Kendall may not live because amniotic fluid had been leaking throughout the pregnancy, undetected. It upset Desiree that they kept speaking these faithless words over their child. Kendall lived only one day before he passed away. Desiree was very angry about this loss and did not hold the baby as much as she had held Kyle, because she did not want to get attached to him.

Desiree did everything she could to not have to go through planning burial services for yet another baby. This time, she planned a very intimate service. Kyle's service was largely attended and she did not want that for Kendall. "I had an autopsy [performed] with this second child because I could not get over the fact that this had happened again; I wanted to know what happened," says Desiree.

While carrying Kendall, God had told Desiree, "If you give this baby back to me, I will use this situation for my glory." She thought that maybe God meant that once the baby arrived, they were to christen Him; but she had no idea what He really meant. She has often wondered why He allowed her to go through this experience.

Desiree went through periods of depression, and for about a week or two, she needed help because she would not shower, dress, or take care of her children. She did not have a desire to take care of her home or anything else. She ate whatever she wanted. Some days, she would say,

"I'm not getting up, I'm not doing anything...and I dare you (Kenneth) to say something about it."

This scenario happened off and on and then she moved into a state of functioning depression. Desiree said, "It felt like the pain was so excruciating and overbearing and people didn't understand. It was not a good time." She did a lot of research after the second loss, to find out why it had happened. She thought that her doctor was leaving something out and not telling her.

Although Desiree was mad at God about the loss of her baby, she still kept seeking Him. She read the Bible, watched spiritual videos, and tried to go to church because these practices were her lifeline. She felt that she had to stay close to God because she was going through a lot and there were so many things that she didn't understand. She wanted to allow God to heal her anger and bitterness but she did not know how He would do it.

Seeing babies and pregnant women was difficult for Desiree. She felt angry and sad. When her nephew came to their house with his wife, who was *very* pregnant at the time, it felt almost unbearable for Desiree to watch her walking around. At one point, Desiree started to yell at her. Kenneth recognized that the real issue was that Desiree was having a hard time seeing his wife pregnant while Desiree was still grieving the loss of her son. He brought this to her attention and she burst out crying while Kenneth hugged and consoled her.

Not long after the loss of Kendall, Desiree found out that she was pregnant once more. This pregnancy was unplanned and Desiree thought she was crazy for being careless and getting pregnant again. As with her past pregnancies, there were a lot of precautions taken to give her the best possible chance of delivering a healthy baby. Desiree was shocked to find out that she was carrying twins this time! She immediately remembered the prophecy spoken to her after the loss of her first son. Both Desiree and Kenneth were excited to be having twins.

The labor and delivery process was normal and Desiree had a cesarean delivery. On December 7, 2007, Korey and Kamden Smith were born. The first baby came out screaming. The second baby was taken out of the room and Desiree didn't know what had happened. . Both babies had to stay in the Neonatal Intensive Care Unit (NICU) for a couple of weeks because of their low birth weight and because one of the babies was not eating. Desiree was amazed that Kamden looked like Kyle, her first son, who had passed away. Both babies were fair skinned and had round faces. Korey's appearance favored Kendall, the second son they had lost. It was as if God were restoring the couple's losses.

Today, when Desiree looks at her twins, they remind her of the sons she lost. She does not visit the deceased children's gravesites because she does not want to open those wounds up again. But she says there is not a time when she doesn't think about them. "They are still in my heart and I look forward to seeing them when I make it to heaven," she says.

Looking back, Desiree realizes that she did not allow herself to grieve properly for either loss. She did some therapeutic journaling and read a lot of books on pain, but nothing on grief. "I have a passion for people who experience that type of loss," she says. When asked what she wants other women to know, Desiree says, "Some way or somehow, there is purpose in what you went through. You may not know what it is, but just continue to hold on, trust God, and know that all things are working together for your good. We have to look at it as an honor...like how He (God) chose Mary to birth Jesus. He chose us to house the babies He wanted to go back to Him."

24

Maya's Story

Aaron and Maya's story started in 2006, when Maya was a senior in high school. Aaron was home from college and a mutual friend set them up on a blind date. Neither of them was excited about the date, but obliged. She had no clue they would have such a strong connection and would be inseparable from that day forward.

They dated for five years prior to getting married in July of 2011. Aaron and Maya decided to enjoy their time together as husband and wife for a while before starting a family. At the time, Maya was taking birth control pills, which caused her to have sporadic menstrual cycles. Missing a cycle was nothing surprising for Maya, so when she went to the doctor for an annual physical, she did not understand why the doctor wanted to perform a pregnancy test.

Maya told the doctor she was wasting her time, and she was not prepared for the news the doctor shared with her when she returned to the room. "Congratulations!" said the doctor. "For what?" Maya asked. "You are pregnant!" said the doctor. Maya was totally shocked. She was six weeks pregnant. No wonder she had been so sleepy over the past few weeks.

Once she left the doctor's office, Maya called Aaron to let him know she had some news to share with him. She wanted to wait until he returned home, but he wanted to know right then. When Maya told him she was pregnant, Aaron's response was, "How did that happen?" He was just as shocked as she was.

After recovering from the initial shock, both were happy to have a little one on the way. The beginning of the pregnancy was uneventful and they started making baby plans. At about three months, Aaron and Maya went to an appointment to find out the sex of the baby and they were told they were having a girl. Aaron was excited to be having a girl and took extra precautions to make sure Maya was not overexerting herself or doing anything that would harm his baby girl. Their pastor, on the other hand, was pretty sure they were going to have a boy. They let him think as he wanted, but assured him that the doctor confirmed the baby's sex as a girl. Aaron and Maya chose to name the baby Madelyn.

At the same appointment, when they found out the sex of the baby, Aaron and Maya were also told that the doctors saw something wrong with the baby's heart and that there was a possibility the baby would have Downs Syndrome. They were offered the opportunity to have an amniocentesis to better determine the health of the baby, but they declined. They decided they would believe God for healing and no matter what, would love the baby as she was.

At the five-month mark, Aaron and Maya were informed that the baby was underweight, not getting nutrients, and that there was a kink in the umbilical cord. Maya was sent to a specialist in Jackson, Mississippi that was about one-and-a-half hours away from her home. After being examined, Maya was told she would need to take steroids to build up baby Madelyn's lungs, in the event of pre-term labor.

As a result of the rounds of steroids, Maya experienced quite a bit of fluid build-up in her body. She was later told that she had Preeclampsia, which could have also contributed to the fluid build-up. At a routine OB/GYN visit, Maya's doctor noticed that her blood pressure was high. She was prescribed medication and instructed to monitor her blood pressure at home.

One day, Maya did a blood pressure check and noticed that her numbers were high. She told her mother, who told her they needed to get to the hospital immediately. Upon arrival, Maya was placed in Labor and Delivery for a check-up. The check-up revealed that Maya's blood pressure was at stroke level and that she was leaking amniotic fluid. She was placed in an ambulance and transported to Jackson, Mississippi, with her family trailing closely behind. She preferred to ride in the ambulance alone because she did not want anyone to make her more nervous than she already was.

Much of what happened after arriving at the hospital in Jackson is a blur to Maya. She was informed that she would need to have an emergency C-Section. Then, unbeknownst to her, she started having severe, long-lasting seizures. Maya later learned that she had a seizure and then woke up and asked everyone why they were looking at her funny. She also remembers telling everyone, "Don't worry...God's got me." After an hour-long seizure, Aaron was staring at May with eyes as big as saucers.

The next day, Maya woke up and every part of her body was in pain. She asked Aaron what was going on and he was stunned that she had no clue what had happened. Maya was not even aware that she had given birth; in fact, she thought she was still pregnant. Aaron informed her that she had given birth to a baby boy, just as their pastor had predicted. "You really don't know what happened?" He asked. "You almost died. You had four bad seizures."

As Aaron showed Maya pictures of the baby, she was in shock that she had given birth to Mason and not Madelyn. The baby looked just like his father. The joy of having the baby was overshadowed by the news that little Mason was in the neonatal intensive care unit (NICU). Since Maya had been only six months pregnant when she gave birth, Mason's lungs and intestines had not fully developed.

Maya was so distraught over Mason's condition that she asked for her fallopian tubes to be tied. She thought the pre-term delivery that caused his condition was all her fault because she suffers from a genetic disorder called neurofibromatosis. The doctor would not consent to a tubal ligation, assuring Aaron and Maya that the pre-term delivery was not the result of her disorder and that, in fact, it happens often. Mason was given medication to help him develop. Unfortunately, a blood vessel burst in his head. Doctors told them that if Mason did survive, he would have complications and would need to have a stint surgery around age one.

Each time Maya held and gazed at her baby, she did not see anything wrong with him. All she could see was an amazing blessing that God had blessed her and Aaron with. Everyone kept telling her that Mason was sick, but she could not see it. Now, looking back, Maya wonders if she did not *want* to see it.

After five days in the hospital, Maya was discharged. There were no rooms available at the Ronald McDonald House, so they could not stay close to Mason. While they waited for a room to free up there, Aaron and Maya decided to travel the one-and-a-half hour drive back home. Neither of them wanted to leave Mason alone, but Aaron wanted to make sure Maya was safe as well, for fear of her having a seizure again.

Maya called the hospital several times a day to check in on Mason. Every day, except for two, the couple made the long drive to see their baby in person. At first, it seemed like Mason was getting better. He was taken off oxygen and was breathing on his own. Then, all of a sudden, his health seemed to deteriorate quickly.

During this time, family and friends supported them from near and far. One day, they got a call from the hospital, informing them that Mason might not make it and that they should come see him one last time. When they arrived, Maya held him, talked to him, and took pictures of him. She found herself singing these words to Mason: "God wants to heal you everywhere you hurt."

Maya's pastor had always told his congregation that words are important. In that moment, as she sang those words to Mason, she finally understood what her pastor had meant. She felt that God was telling her that whether Mason was healed on earth or in heaven, he was going to be all right.

Aaron and Maya struggled with whether or not to leave the hospital that night. The drive back home was very long and quiet. Once the couple arrived home, Maya said her prayers and went to sleep. At 6:52 a.m. the telephone rang. It was the hospital, informing them that Mason had passed away four minutes earlier. Maya dropped the phone. Aaron retrieved it and spoke with the nurse. Not knowing what to do, Maya got very quiet. She had thoughts that she should have stayed at the hospital.

Next, they called their parents and shared the terrible news with them. Aaron drove to Jackson to sign the death certificate. He told Maya she should stay home because he thought this task would be too hard on her. While he was at the hospital, Maya began making arrangements for Mason's funeral. The former mayor of Mississippi attended Maya's church and offered to pay for the funeral. Her pastor offered to have the services at their church and Maya's cousin volunteered to perform the service. The couple was showered with love and support.

On the day of the funeral service, only two days after Mason passed away, it was pouring rain. The gloomy weather matched Aaron and Maya's feelings. Maya cried during the entire service and Aaron zoned out. They were amazed at the number of people who came out in the rain to express their condolences. At one point, no longer able to keep his emotions under control, Aaron fell to the ground. A scream rose up from the inside of him and he broke down crying. Maya had never seen him like that. After the service was over, Maya's pastor told her that she was having a "Job experience" and recommended that she read that book of the Bible when she had time.

Ironically, the day after the funeral service was Maya's birthday. She and Aaron went out to eat, but Maya was in no mood to celebrate. She just did not feel right celebrating another year of life, knowing Mason had lost his life. They decided to take the food home and watch a movie. Aaron tried to lift Maya's mood by selecting a comedy for them to watch, but she fell asleep in his lap.

The first Sunday after Mason's funeral, Maya went to church, as normal. But this Sunday was different. Maya was different. She wore black and white, walked down to the front of the church, and sat on the first pew. Full of anger, Maya did not listen to one word the pastor preached. She felt like the devil was sitting besides her asking, "Why are you even here? You gonna sit here and serve a man that would give you something and take it away?" Maya thought, "You're right. What is the point in living right and doing right, when He snatches life from you?"

Maya hated God in that moment and she didn't care. She could not wrap her mind around how a loving God could knowingly allow something so horrible to happen. Her mother noticed that she was not looking like herself and asked if Maya was okay. Not wanting to be bothered, Maya said, "I'm fine." She made it home, took off her shoes, and immediately hit the floor. She started to weep and asked God to forgive her for having such evil thoughts.

After pulling herself together, Maya still questioned God about why this horrible thing had happened to them. She told God, "You tell me everything about everybody else, why won't you tell me about my situation?" The only answer she received was that God was telling her that she would not be able to handle His answer.

One day, while in the shower, Maya had had enough and she cried out to God one last time. Aaron was in the next room, working out, and wondered whom she was talking to. She begged God to give answer her about why He had taken Mason from them. The answer Maya heard from God was: "Who do you think you are, that you're not going to go through anything difficult? I gave my only son to save your life. He was beaten and he didn't say anything. They talked about him and his flesh hung from his body. You go through a little something and you are complaining about it. So don't ask me, 'Why me?'...Ask 'why him?'"

This answer left Maya in awe and all she could do was weep. She felt selfish. Yes, losing Mason hurt and she wanted her child to be there with them, but she acknowledged that we all have to go through difficult times. "God didn't say that life on earth would be easy," she said to herself. She finally took her pastor up on his suggestion and started reading the book of Job. As she read it, she could totally relate to Job's situation.

Although Maya received an answer from God that brought her a better sense of understanding, it still did not take away the pain of losing her child. She and Aaron did not talk about their loss much. He buried himself in work, and Maya flipped from snapping at people just for looking at her, to crying. Her aunt told her she needed to just get over it. Maya could not believe that someone could be so insensitive.

Eventually, Aaron told her she needed to get some help, so she went to the doctor. The doctor prescribed some medication that calmed her down. After taking it for a short period of time, Maya's pharmacist told her she did not need the medication anymore, so she weaned herself off of it against the doctor's recommendation and started relying on prayer. She wondered if Aaron blamed her for the loss of Mason. When she asked him about it, he told her that he did not and that they had no control over what had happened.

Even though he did not blame Maya, he still did not open up to her about his pain. Dealing with loss was not something Aaron did well. He still had not completely dealt with the death of his grandmother who had raised him and was like a mother to him. Losing Mason was another loss that he pushed down. Maya felt like that his suppression put a shield between the two of them. Surprisingly, when Maya asked him if he was open to having more children, he said, "Why not? God blessed us once. He can do it again."

Throughout the entire grief process, Maya's best friend was a huge support. "She was my rock," Maya said. Although she and Maya had been pregnant at the same time, her friend did everything she could to minimize any pain Maya experienced from watching her friend continue with her pregnancy; including not inviting her to her baby shower.

At first, Maya was mad at her best friend for not inviting her, but in time, she realized how thoughtful it was for her friend to consider her feelings. She told Maya, "I would not put you in that position." Other friends and family were very supportive, as well. Her co-workers even took turns preparing food and delivering it to the couple's home so they would not have to cook.

For eight months, Maya was off work as her doctors monitored her for seizures. Her driver's license was suspended during this time and friends and family had to drive her anywhere she needed to go. There were many days when Maya did not want to be bothered. She shut everybody out. She did not want to think about, hear about, or talk about her loss. At one point, she took more Zoloft than she was prescribed so that she would not have to feel anything.

Over a year after Mason passed away, Maya's mother drove her to a follow-up appointment in Jackson. When they stopped along the way at the gas station, Maya started browsing through the photos on her mother's phone. She came across a photo of Mason and, for the first time, she could see what everybody else saw. Mason was sick. She cried, as for the first time, she was able to see and acknowledge it.

Although Maya thinks about Mason on a daily basis and misses him dearly, she has regained a strong faith and trust in God. She still believes He is good and has good things in store for her.

25

Trent and Stephanie's Story

Trent and Stephanie had known each other for years as friends, prior to getting married. Shortly after their 2004 marriage, they conceived their first child. Stephanie wrapped a newborn outfit in a cute little box to let Trent know they were having a baby. Of course, they were excited, as were their family members.

At Stephanie's first prenatal doctor's appointment, the doctor examined her and informed her that she had a tilted uterus. At this realization, the doctor told her, "Your baby could fall out...so we will monitor you and see how far you get with this." Stephanie was unsure what to do with this news and the severity of his words did not really register with her. When the doctor sent her home, she assumed everything would be fine.

At Stephanie's next visit with this doctor, he checked her hormone levels. He asked her to come back the next day, to check them again and see if her numbers were going up or down because, he said, he had a feeling that there was "nothing there." Still new to this whole prenatal process, Stephanie did not think to ask questions about what the doctor meant when he said "nothing there."

Stephanie went back to the doctor as she was instructed to do and, to her horror, she was no longer pregnant after eleven-and-a-half weeks of gestation. She did not have any bleeding to give her a clue that anything was wrong, so, of course, she was dumbfounded and confused. The doctor did not have an exact answer as to how this miscarriage had happened, but he did say that it could have happened one day while she was using the restroom. Her first thought was that this must be God's way of punishing her for the abortion she had many years earlier.

She left the doctor's office, went home, and told her husband and immediate family the news. Trent and Stephanie did not take time to process what had happened or even grieve the loss of their baby. They both went right back to work and moved on with life as usual. Grieving was not an option for Stephanie, as she had many family members depending on her to be strong.

After the loss of the baby, Stephanie thought that she and her husband should attempt to get pregnant again pretty quickly. So later that same year, they conceived again. This time, the same doctor who had treated her for the first pregnancy put Stephanie on home bed rest, at about four-and-a-half months' gestation.

Stephanie started to have some cramping and bleeding and immediately went to the doctor. The examination revealed that she had once again lost the baby. Of course, Trent and Stephanie were devastated by the loss of their second child. However, instead of taking time to grieve, they joined their family and friends on a three-day camping trip, as if all was well with the world. Stephanie could tell that her husband Trent was struggling inside, but once again, she felt that grieving was not an option because she still had people depending on her to be strong.

After the second loss, Stephanie wondered, "What is wrong with me? Am I being punished?" She felt like she had done things the right way, by waiting until marriage to have children; so she could not understand why God was allowing this to happen. For a long time after the second loss, Stephanie did not want to be intimate with her husband. She felt horrible that she did not want to be touched by him, but it had nothing to do with him; she was just gripped with fear.

About one year later, Trent and Stephanie found out that they were pregnant for the third time. Stephanie was excited and not excited at the same time, because she was fearful, wondering if she would miscarry again. Her husband could not get excited at all, in the beginning. After they had made it through the third and fourth months of pregnancy, he then allowed himself to get excited.

Trent and Stephanie were enjoying the pregnancy and the excitement was building within the family. There was hope again, since Stephanie had made it farther in this pregnancy than in the past two. The couple completed a baby registry and Stephanie's mother purchased a crib in preparation for their little bundle of joy. They continued to see the same doctor who had assisted them through the first two pregnancies, with no thought yet as to why he had not offered some type of solution to their repeated losses.

One day, while at home, Stephanie went to the restroom and noticed an unusual, clear fluid leakage. She called the doctor and they instructed her to immediately go to the emergency room, fearing that her water had broken. Once Stephanie and Trent arrived at the emergency room, the nurses examined Stephanie. Being able to feel the baby moving and hearing the heartbeat reassured her.

After it was determined that the baby was fine, the doctor informed Stephanie that she would need to stay overnight. The next day, when he returned, he broke the news to Stephanie that she would need to stay in the hospital and be on bed rest until the baby was delivered. This was during the Christmas holiday season, which is Stephanie's favorite time of year, so she was a bit saddened by the news. But she and Trent were willing to do whatever was necessary to ensure a healthy delivery.

The doctor assured Stephanie that even though her water was leaking, if she ingested enough fluids she could continue to build up the fluid in her water sack. She stayed in a very large, comfortable room, which accommodated her and allowed Trent to spend the night whenever he wanted. At this time, Trent was in school, so he could not be there for Stephanie as much as he wanted, but her mother visited her every day. This was a very humbling time for Stephanie, because she was unable to do anything but move from her bed to the potty chair that was placed next to her bed. Each day, Trent or her mother bathed Stephanie from head to toe, while she was lying on the bed.

On Christmas Eve, just as they hit the five-month mark, as Stephanie was watching television, she felt some mild cramping. She contacted the nurse on duty and explained her symptoms, and was given Tylenol to relieve the discomfort. The next day, Stephanie and Trent enjoyed Christmas at the hospital. Stephanie's family came, bearing gifts. The doctor even made an appearance on Christmas day, to make sure that things were progressing normally and that they could hear the baby's heartbeat. Everything seemed fine.

The day went by without event. However, later that evening, the cramping returned. Once again, Stephanie notified the nurse and was given more Tylenol to relieve the symptoms. She trusted the nurse's judgment and expertise, so she did not question why she was being given a pain reliever again. Early the next morning, around two o'clock, Stephanie went to use the restroom while Trent slept. As she used the restroom, she felt something coming out of her. As she looked down, she saw her baby but it was still attached. She yelled for Trent to wake up and call the nurse.

At this point, she still felt like there was a chance the baby might live. The nurses arrived and laid Stephanie back down on the bed, while she waited expectantly to hear the sound of her baby crying. But she never heard a sound. She was taken down to the operating room, where the baby's umbilical cord was cut. She was still unaware of what exactly was going on. She asked Trent to call all of their family and close friends to let them know what was happening.

Finally, her doctor arrived and said, "I'm so sorry." A few minutes later, the male nurse who was assisting them asked if they would like to know the sex of the baby. Stephanie was too numb to answer, so Trent answered, "Yes" for both of them. The nurse informed them that Stephanie had delivered a baby boy. He asked if they would like to see the baby. Both Trent and Stephanie agreed that they would; however, once the baby was brought into the room, Stephanie lost it and was unable look at him.

Trent, on the other hand, held the baby, bravely opened up the blanket, and looked at him from head to toe. To this day, Stephanie still regrets that she did not look at her son. To make matters worse, Stephanie had to have a dilation and curettage (DNC), a procedure in which small pieces of placenta are removed from the uterus after childbirth.

During this time at the hospital, Stephanie and Trent's pastor reached out to Stephanie, to console and comfort her and to provide her with some Scriptural strength. But she was not open to hearing anything about God at that moment. As nicely as she could, Stephanie told him, "Bishop, thank you for being here, but I think your work is done." She felt like no one who was trying to comfort them could comprehend what she was feeling on the inside. This pregnancy had been something they had really wanted, and this had been their third try.

After finally returning home, Stephanie was home alone one day and happened to sneeze. When she did so, she felt a gush of blood come out. She just assumed that it was the normal bleeding that occurs after the birth of a child. So she went to the restroom and began to feel weak. As she urinated, the blood continued to pour out of her like water. Realizing something must be wrong, she called the doctor's office. The response she received was, "That's normal, since you just lost a baby and had a DNC...just keep an eye on it."

Still feeling that something was not right; Stephanie decided that she needed to go to the emergency room. Home alone and unable to drive, she called her mother to transport her to the hospital. She had to figure out how to get to the door with all of the blood flowing out of her. The situation worsened as the bleeding was coupled with severe abdominal pain. Stephanie crawled to the door to let her mother in. Her mother was shocked at the trail of blood on the floor, leading from the restroom to the front door.

Trent met them at the hospital. Inside the emergency room, the staff told Stephanie to have a seat and they would get to her soon. She attempted to let them know that she needed immediate attention, but she was still told to wait. After what seemed like a long time, Stephanie was finally taken back to have her vitals checked. As she sat in the chair, a lady behind her called the nurse taking the vitals, to tell her that Stephanie had a puddle of blood on the floor beneath her. Immediately, they put Stephanie on the gurney and took her back for an ultrasound, to determine the source of the bleeding. It was determined that she had a fibroid tumor. The doctors were dumbfounded that after three pregnancies and many ultrasounds this had not been previously discovered.

The blood loss was so great that before they could move forward with treatment, Stephanie needed a blood transfusion. Of course she did not want this, but she had no other choice. For another week and a half, Stephanie remained in the hospital and underwent a uterine fibroid embolization to shrink the fibroids. She was told, "You may either be sterile for the rest of your life, or this procedure could cause the fibroid to shrink and come out on its own." The thought of not being able to have kids scared Stephanie and Trent, but they felt there was no other option at this point, so they agreed to go through with the procedure.

After it was complete, all Stephanie could think about was the word "sterile." Even though they had given her two potential outcomes of the surgical procedure, that was the only word that kept ringing in her mind. She could not stop feeling like she was being punished for everything wrong she had ever done. She was concerned about what her husband would think. The enemy started to taunt her, saying, "You could have had a child a long time ago...she would probably be twelve years old now." Stephanie felt so empty; like she could not fight for herself against these spiritual attacks. She felt like she had nothing left and did not even know what to ask for anymore in prayer. "I just kept wondering, 'Am I that bad? I'm living for you, God,'" she said. She found herself thinking about people she knew who were not living for God and how life appeared to be going well for them. Although she knew that there was a certain amount of struggle that comes along with living a life for Christ, she felt like she could not get a break. "I felt like an orphaned child who was left alone with no one to pull strength from," recalls Stephanie.

As for emotional support, Stephanie said no one really asked her how she was feeling. Her family was physically present with her, but she received no emotional support. They seemed to think that feeding her would make her feel better; but she never had the opportunity to talk about her grief. After just two weeks, Stephanie went back to work because she did not know what to do.

Eventually, Stephanie returned to the doctor for a follow-up visit from her surgery. The doctor told her that the fibroid was gone and that there was no sign at all that she could not have children. "It's amazing!" he said. Stephanie was quick to say, "No, that's just God!" She would not allow the credit to be given to anyone or anything else but God. To this day, Stephanie still has a sticker on her board at work, to remind her of the day that she received this miraculous news.

During this season, Trent and Stephanie's marital relationship began to suffer because Stephanie was unable to connect anymore. She felt like she did not have anything left to give. "I'd been through too much," says Stephanie. "I was so numb." It was a hard time for them. It took approximately two years for her to release the fear of being intimate with her husband.

To add to their feelings of emptiness, loss, and disappointment, Trent and Stephanie later found out that the baby boy they were told they delivered was actually a baby girl. This information came out by chance, when Stephanie was talking to a different doctor who was reviewing their medical records. Now bewilderment and confusion were added to the long list of emotions the couple already was struggling with. How could this be? They had named their baby boy and mourned his passing. Now what were they supposed to do? Stephanie knows God kept her from losing her mind throughout these years of grief, loss, and confusion.

During Stephanie's tough period of grief, the mothers of their church came to the house. While Stephanie lay on the sofa, they sat on the floor around her. They brought her food, rubbed her feet, sang, laughed, cried, and shared Scriptures and stories of how they overcame hardships in their lives. Stephanie felt special knowing they had taken time to do this for her.

Stephanie, who had been a powerful praise and worship leader at her church, no longer had a desire to sing. She became disrespectful to the mothers of the church, for whom she had once had the utmost respect. She would not hold her tongue and had no fear of consequences. She began to feel like it didn't even matter if she was saved anymore.

Next came a silent, very painful period of grieving, when Stephanie felt like she had a hole in her heart. In addition to the grief from the loss of her babies, Stephanie's unresolved grief from the passing of her father a few years earlier resurfaced. One day while at church, a lady in leadership, who also happened to be a counselor, asked if she could speak with Stephanie. Resistant to anything anyone had to say, and not wanting another person to pray for her, Stephanie reluctantly walked over to the woman. After just a few minutes of being ministered to, Stephanie began to release all of her pent-up feelings, through a torrent of tears. This woman was the first person to break through the stonewall Stephanie had put up to keep people away. The healing process had finally begun. She was able to get to the point of being transparent, and she no longer felt the need to mask her feelings and say everything was okay when it wasn't.

As is common, months after losing her third baby, Stephanie continued to receive expectant mother mail. Her first instinct was to toss it all in the trash each time it arrived. However, Stephanie sensed the Holy Spirit leading her to keep all of these items in a box. Although she did not understand the purpose for this, she obeyed. Also around this time, someone told Stephanie about a book titled *Supernatural Child Birth* by Jackie Mize, which she purchased.

In the book, Mize told her own story of having approximately six miscarriages and eventually going on to deliver three or four children. Stephanie related to many of the experiences the author described and often became very emotional while reading. She followed the book's suggestion to speak Scriptures over her womb, before trying to get pregnant again.

Stephanie had a strong desire for Trent to read the book, as well, so she purchased it on CD and played it in their bedroom each evening while they prepared for bed. She set the CD player to the repeat function so that the Scriptures would flow through their room over and over. She also read the Scriptures daily, while at work; speaking them over her womb.

The tables had turned in Trent and Stephanie's relationship. Now he was fearful to be intimate with his wife because he did not want her to go through that pain again. But Stephanie's faith had been stirred up and she became angry at Trent. "So when are we going to trust God?" she asked. She could not have spoken these words two years earlier. The couple was eventually able to be intimate again, but trepidation now joined them in the bedroom.

As time went on, Stephanie selected a new doctor and was excited when he required her to take a series of tests that she had never been required to take before. Her hope for a healthy pregnancy was renewed. At the first visit, the doctor told Stephanie that she needed to go have some blood work done on the first day of her next menstrual cycle. So when her cycle started, Stephanie called doctor because her bleeding was sporadic. "Do me a favor...can you come to the office?" the doctor asked. "I want you to take a pregnancy test." Stephanie was caught off guard and made it very clear to the doctor that she was not pregnant because she knew that the moments of intimacy between her and Trent had been infrequent. Driving thirty minutes to take a pregnancy test that she knew would be negative was not on Stephanie's list of things to do that day. She compromised with the doctor, who by now was laughing at Stephanie's resistance. She drove to a nearby store and purchased a pregnancy test to take back to work with her.

Stephanie went into the restroom at work and followed the steps on the pregnancy test. While waiting for the results, which she knew were going to be negative, she looked at herself in the mirror, walked around, and ran the water; anything to keep her busy while waiting the few minutes for the test results. After checking her watch and realizing that it was time for the results to appear, she walked over to where the applicator was resting. She thought her eyes were deceiving her. "That test was so positive," Stephanie said. "It was clear as day." She put her hand on her hips, looked up at God, and said out loud, "You have got to be FREAKIN' kidding me!" She knew the people outside of the door must have been wondering what she was doing in there. Stephanie could not stop looking at the test; she could not believe her eyes. After stuffing the test and all of its components back in her purse, she went back to her desk to call the doctor.

"Dr. Castillo, I have something to tell you," Stephanie's explained. Dr. Castillo, already knowing what Stephanie was going to say, replied, "Tell me...humor me." Stephanie forced the words, "It says that I'm pregnant," out of her mouth. "So what do I do?" she asked. "You need to make an appointment to come in and see me," said the doctor.

After hanging up the phone, Stephanie did not call Trent right away. She was unable to get excited about the news, so she waited about an hour or two before calling him at work. As they discussed this miraculous conception of sorts, neither of them had any excitement in their voices. But in the back of her mind, Stephanie remembered all of the Scriptures she had prayed over her womb. She felt like God was telling her that He was going to fulfill the promise He had made to her. She felt like He was asking her, "Will you trust me?"

During the visit with Dr. Castillo, Stephanie told her all about the events of her first three pregnancies and how a previous doctor had told her about her tilted cervix. To Stephanie's surprise, this news did not perplex or startle Dr. Castillo at all. It was very clear to the doctor that a Cerclage procedure, in which strong thread is used to stitch the cervix closed, would need to be done, to ensure that the baby would stay inside of Stephanie's womb.

Stephanie vividly remembers the doctor saying, "*When* you get to your twelfth week, we are going to do your Cerclage." The doctor never used the word "if" when referring to the pregnancy and always spoke "life" during every visit, which confirmed for Stephanie, that God was confirming His plan. Not once did the doctor speak anything negative about the pregnancy.

After the Cerclage procedure, Stephanie asked the doctor, "So, what now?"

"Nothing. We just wait," was the doctor's reply.

The doctor mentioned that this procedure greatly reduces the chances of premature birth, but that there are some instances where it still happens. Throughout the pregnancy, Stephanie was in the doctor's office more than usual, so that they could keep a close watch on her.

As the pregnancy progressed to its fifth month, Stephanie eventually became excited. However, Trent was not feeling the joy of the pregnancy. He had experienced too many disappointments, and it was not until Stephanie was approximately seven months pregnant that he was able to join in on the excitement.

Another test of Stephanie's faith during this pregnancy was to not let fear creep in. She had to daily push away feelings of fear that would attempt to rise up against her. God sent several cheerleaders across her path to encourage her, as she neared the finish line. "It was like running a race...literally," she said. "And it was if they were encouraging me along the way, saying, 'I've got some water for you. You want some water? Drink some water 'cause you need some water!'"

Stephanie had very few complications during the pregnancy. At one point, she had some minor spotting and when she contacted the doctor's office, they assured her that everything was fine. In addition to the regular doctor's visits, Stephanie was scheduled for antenatal testing three times a week. This is a process where a monitor is placed on the mother's stomach to detect fetal movement.

She also had encounters with several earthly angels, in the form of nurses. These interactions confirmed even further to Stephanie that God was with her during this process. During one visit to the antenatal testing unit, one of the nurses made it a point to request to work with her. She told Stephanie, "There is something about you. I see you... just know that He (God) has you in the palm of His hand." She called Stephanie periodically, to follow up and to make sure that she was coming in for her testing dates.

At approximately thirty-seven weeks, Stephanie had severe edema. She asked the doctor if there was any way she could deliver early. After measuring her stomach, which measured at forty-two weeks, Dr. Castillo felt sympathy for her and agreed to do a C-section.

Stephanie delivered a healthy baby boy. After the delivery, Stephanie and Trent could not stop staring into Adan's little face. They were amazed that he was finally there; after all they had been through. God had kept his promise to them. A few days later, Stephanie was allowed to finally leave the hospital for the last time and to take her bundle of joy home.

Today, Stephanie still gets teary eyed when someone else has a loss. She also has feelings of sadness when she sees a newborn child, as it causes her to wonder about the children she lost and what they would look like or how old they would be now.

However, despite all she has been through, Stephanie wants other women who are reading this book and have experienced a loss to know that there is hope after the loss. Her words of advice to you are:

> *"Looking back on everything that I have gone through, I realize that I had to go through it then in order for me to help someone else. I learned that it's okay to suffer loss, grieve, and allow God to restore you back to your place in Him. God really showed me His sovereignty in all of this and how we're not anointed for easy, but we're anointed for hard. I knew that somehow, my miracle and my breakthrough were going to spring forth from my pain. I'm learning daily as the song says, 'If I can help somebody as I pass along, if I can cheer somebody with a word or song, if I can help somebody from doing wrong, then my living shall not be in vain!'"*

Epilogue

At the time of the writing of this book, it has been five years since we lost Riley. So much has happened in our lives since then. Our oldest daughter, Diamond, has graduated from undergraduate college and is now in a graduate program in another state. Sydney has graduated from high school and is now in college studying cosmetology, and Noelle is in her final year of middle school.

Greg and I celebrated twenty years of marriage with an intimate vow-renewal ceremony. All of our children, including Riley, were a part of the ceremony. In her honor, we had two large letter 'R' initials attached to the awning where our vows were recited. Also, to honor her and our other loved ones who could not join in the celebration, Greg and I lit candles.

In the wake of our painful experience, my anger with God had caused me to decide that I would not finish the doctorate degree I knew He was leading me to earn. I eventually surrendered and returned to school. After a one-year break to grieve and re-calibrate, I completed my dissertation and graduated in May 2015. It was bittersweet because Riley was not able to join us in the celebration.

I went on to become licensed as a Marriage and Family Therapist (LMFT), a journey I had started long before we lost Riley, and opened Maple Leaf Counseling Services. My private counseling practice specializes in counseling women, men, and families who have lost infant children due to stillbirth, illness, pre-term labor, and miscarriage. I have also started a support group at our church for women who have experienced pregnancy and infant loss.

I named the practice Maple Leaf because while I was in the hospital after losing Riley, a sign was placed outside my door. It pictured a maple leaf with a teardrop in it, to alert the nursing staff that a stillbirth had occurred. The sign is placed there to prompt them to be sensitive to the needs of the mother and family who have just experienced such a traumatic loss. That act of sensitivity and kindness really touched me.

I have learned that infant loss is an unspoken pain that many women and families live with daily. It is a secret club that no one talks about because its grieving members did not ask for membership, and they all hope that no more members are initiated. For some, the silence is due to the shame of a perceived failure; and for others, it is a wound that is too painful to peel the scab from. I want to break the walls of silence and open up the dialogue about our pain, grief, paths to healing, and the lives of our little ones who did exist and still matter.

This grief journey has taught me that healing is not a destination but a lifelong journey. I have learned that months after a loss, when family has gone home and life is supposed to return to "normal" is when a card, phone call, or text is needed the most. I did not know how to be emotionally or physically available for others during times of grief prior to losing Riley. I now know how to live out the words of II Corinthians 1:3-4: "Blessed be the God and Father of our Lord Jesus Christ, the Father of mercies and God of all comfort, who comforts us in all our tribulation, that we may be able to comfort those who are in any trouble, with the comfort with which we ourselves are comforted by God."

Each year on Riley's birthday, our family visits Riley's gravesite. It always amazes us that each year, more and more headstones are added to the baby cemetery. Then, we share a meal together that we think Riley would want to eat at the age she would have been. We also either bake or purchase a cake and sing "Happy Birthday" to her.

We have learned how to incorporate Riley into the fabric of our home by hanging up the family picture that we took on Father's Day, when I was pregnant with her. I have also taken a few items out of her keepsake box and placed them around the house, along with her initials from our vow renewal ceremony. It is important to me to never forget, or let others forget, that she did exist, she mattered, and that she was loved.

Over the years, I have found myself struggling with how to answer people when they ask how many children I have. Whenever I forget to say *four,* I still feel guilty that I have left her out. I have finally decided that I am more concerned with how uncomfortable I feel when I forget to acknowledge her life, than I am about how uncomfortable others are when I do. I have gone through several versions of how to answer that question, and now I just say, "I have four daughters; a twenty-six-year old, a twenty-year-old, a thirteen--year-old, and a five-year-old in heaven." Sometimes the conversation ends there because people get uncomfortable, and sometimes it opens up the dialogue about experiences of loss that others have had.

Seeing pregnant women has gotten easier over the years. I still seem to stop in my tracks when I see a woman who is very pregnant and think of my experience. I also say a prayer that she does not experience loss as I did. It took me four years to attend my first baby shower and it was not so bad. There is still a part of me that feels incomplete without the experience of delivering Riley healthy and whole, and I guess that will always be there. When I see children who are near the age Riley would have been, I stop and lament over the experiences we will never have with her. Although I am caught off guard by grief every now and then, I have many more good days than bad.

It is my hope that this book will instill hope in families who are hopeless and in a dark place due to the loss of their child and all of the hopes and dreams that were attached to it. Just as He has done for us, I pray that God blesses you according to Isaiah 61:3: "To console those who mourn in Zion, to give them beauty for ashes, the oil of joy for mourning, the garment of praise for the spirit of heaviness; that they may be called trees of righteousness, the planting of the Lord, that He may be glorified."

Appendix A

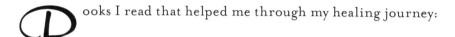Booooks I read that helped me through my healing journey:

- I will Carry You: the sacred dance of grief and joy by Angie Smith

- Love, Mom: a mother's journey from loss to hope by Cynthia Baseman

- Between a Rock and a Grace Place: divine surprises in the tight spots of life by Carol Kent

- When I Lay My Isaac Down: unshakable faith in unthinkable circumstances by Carol Kent

- From Mourning to Morning: discovering the healing power of God's love to take you from grief to glory by Harry & Cheryl Salem

- When Life Hurts: finding hope and healing from the pain you carry by Jimmy Evans

- Tilly by Frank Peretti and Michael W. Smith

96559566R00098

Made in the USA
Columbia, SC
29 May 2018